T0384073

Lean Misconceptions

Why Many Lean Initiatives Fail and How You Can Avoid the Mistakes

Lean Misconceptions

Why Many Lean Initiatives Fail and How You Can Avoid the Mistakes

Cordell Hensley

CRC Press
Taylor & Francis Group
Boca Raton London New York

CRC Press is an imprint of the
Taylor & Francis Group, an **informa** business

A PRODUCTIVITY PRESS BOOK

CRC Press
Taylor & Francis Group
6000 Broken Sound Parkway NW, Suite 300
Boca Raton, FL 33487-2742

© 2018 by Taylor & Francis Group, LLC
CRC Press is an imprint of Taylor & Francis Group, an Informa business

No claim to original U.S. Government works

Printed on acid-free paper

International Standard Book Number-13: 978-1-138-21745-4 (Hardback)

Library of Congress Cataloging-in-Publication Data

Names: Hensley, Cordell, author.
Title: Lean misconceptions : why many lean initiatives fail and how you can avoid the mistakes / Cordell Hensley.
Description: Boca Raton, FL : CRC Press, [2017] | Includes bibliographical references.
Identifiers: LCCN 2016055793| ISBN 9781138217454 (hardback : alk. paper) | ISBN 9781138400153 (ebook)
Subjects: LCSH: Lean manufacturing.
Classification: LCC TS155 .H385 2017 | DDC 658.4/013--dc23
LC record available at https://lccn.loc.gov/2016055793

**Visit the Taylor & Francis Web site at
http://www.taylorandfrancis.com**

**and the CRC Press Web site at
http://www.crcpress.com**

Contents

SECTION II   How the Tools Support the Learning Process

Preface

I wrote this book because I have spent the last decade of my life working in and with organizations that fail to maximize the value in what I teach them. Sure, they have obtained benefits. They have made improvements in their processes. In some cases, I have walked away from a weeklong training event having helped the organization save hundreds of thousands of dollars or pounds in waste. However, in most cases, what they have learned is how to use a specific set of tools. They have their program, either developed in house or usually paid for from an external consultancy.

The programs I have been involved with have almost always had an integral element of learning, on paper at least. However, the organizations and primarily the senior people within the organizations are, in almost all cases, only focused on the return on their investment in the consultancy project. They want to ensure that the money spent on having people in their site is returned in savings from the output of these projects.

It is rare for this not to happen; even today, most organizations have so much waste in their systems that it is reasonably easy to go in, and do some analysis, and find tens if not hundreds of thousands and often millions in savings. However, the reason my industry still exists, the reason why we often get called back to help the same people who have been through this before, is that they are focused too much on the savings or return on investment (ROI) and not enough on the learning.

I am not referring to the learning by their people on how to use the tools, but the learning of their organization as a whole each and every day. They learn how to use the tools and techniques inherent in Lean, in some cases very well. They don't, however, learn to think for themselves and apply the principles behind the tools to innovate and adapt to ever-changing conditions. Arguably, many within my industry are still using the same tools and techniques that they learned years or even decades before.

Not that there is anything wrong with the tools and techniques or that they do not have their place in a Lean organization. They do, but there is more to Lean than a toolbox full of kanban systems, andons, 5S programs, etc. The thinking that sits behind these tools and techniques is far more important than the ability to use them as they come off the shelf.

What is that thinking? Why is it more important? That's why I wrote this book, and if you read on, you will discover exactly that.

What qualifies me to write this book? Not much, to be honest. I spent a few years in Toyota, the company that developed the Toyota Production System, the system that was studied by academics and leaders the world over. Sure, that helps, but I would argue it's not enough. I have spent the last 7 years as a consultant, helping organizations "implement" Lean. Before that, I spent as many years within various organizations using my understanding of the principles of the Toyota Production System to make improvements.

I also spent over a decade in the United States Marine Corps (USMC). An organization famed for its unofficial motto—Improvise, Adapt, and Overcome. An organization that does more with less and has done so since its inception back in 1775; the USMC gets approximately 4% of the defense budget but has almost 14% of the personnel. Wikipedia (2016) states, "The cost per Marine is $20,000 less than the cost of a serviceman from the other services, and the entire force can be used for both hybrid and major combat operations"; I've spent the bulk of my working life in organizations that do more with less. The rest I've spent trying to help companies do more with less.

I studied business, first at the undergraduate level with the University of Phoenix and then at master's level with Manchester Business School, where I earned my MBA. I've read dozens of books on Lean, on business, on organizational behavior, etc.

None of these things individually qualifies me to write this or any other book. However, like Lean, the sum is greater than the parts. I felt that my experience over the past 25 years provides sufficient evidence, albeit mostly anecdotal or provided by fellow colleagues and consultants, to pull together all of my experience and provide my explanation on why so many get it wrong and where the focus should be to get it right.

Author

Cordell Hensley started his career in the USMC as a helicopter mechanic and crew chief. After 11 years of working with TPM, 5S, visualization, standardized work and many other Lean tools, he left the Marines and moved to the UK. There, he joined Toyota in their engine factory in Deeside in North Wales as a Group Leader in production control. He began identifying a culture where ideas could be trialed and learning took place continually.

After spending 8 years in manufacturing, including work in automotive, returnable pallets, electrical steel, and finally potato chips, culminating with the establishment of the logistics function in PepsiCo's Skelmersdale UK crisp factory, he left to become a consultant.

Cordell has been providing continuous improvement consulting for industrial and transactional organizations for 8 years. He's worked in Automotive, Food, Light and Heavy Industrial Goods, FMCG, Pharma, Defense, Machine Shops, Aerospace MRO, Construction, Investment Banking, Call Centers, and Higher Education.

Cordell earned a BSc in Business Management from the University of Phoenix in 2007, a Professional Certificate in Project Management from UoP in 2008 and an MBA from Manchester Business School in 2012. He continues to support the MBS Global MBA with final project supervision.

When not working, Cordell enjoys sailing, chess, reading and the occasional pro-bono consulting engagement with local charities through the Cranfield Trust. He lives on the Wirral peninsula near Liverpool in the UK with his wife and two daughters.

Section I

Misconceptions, Where They Come from, and How to Overcome Them

In this first section, I'd like to start with discussing the various misconceptions within Lean as I see them. While there are surely more than I've identified and some could argue that several could be combined, I believe these are sufficient and unique enough to warrant discussion. These misconceptions are prevalent, even in my own thinking from time to time, and we need to be aware of them as we begin setting the scene for the shift in focus I'll suggest throughout this first section.

Following the misconceptions, I'll provide an overview of how and why companies begin continuous improvement programs and how this affects their results and will, to some extent at least, demonstrate some of the roots of the misconceptions in various scenarios (see Chapter 2).

I then go on to explain a different view or focus for Lean and why I believe it is the best way to truly build the capability and culture so many people talk about (see Chapter 3). Support for this is further given in Chapter 4, which presents a brief history of Lean and continuous improvement more generally. Many, if not all, continuous improvement programs focus on processes and productive output and ignore the development of people. Lean didn't start out that way, but it seems to have ended up here.

In Chapters 5 and 6 of Section I, I delineate the four capabilities as presented by Steven Spear (2009) in his book, *The High-Velocity Edge* and how this focus is far superior to any tool-based program. I then provide a linkage between these four capabilities and the traditional Lean tools that so many are aware of and use daily. The intent is to demonstrate that it is not the application that necessarily needs to change, but the focus. The biggest benefit you will get from reading this book is to understand that we must shift from focusing on benefits and bottom-line results to focusing on people development, on learning, both individually and organizationally. The benefits and bottom-line results will come. Just as Sir Richard Branson (2014) says, "Learn to look after your staff first and the rest will follow."

1

Misconceptions

The focus on removing waste is fundamental within Lean, but it should not be the only objective when beginning on your journey. In fact, I would argue that focusing only on removing waste, like focusing only on the use of the tools and techniques, limits the benefits obtainable by switching to a Lean management system. Removing waste is essential, but it is only a catalyst for the true benefits your organization can achieve when it begins to operate with a true understanding of the value of Lean.

There are at least 10 misconceptions as I see it with Lean as it is applied in most organizations. I will briefly cover these in the rest of this chapter.

The first is the underlying objective of removing people from the organization. Not all organizations have this as their objective, but it has been the case in many of the projects I have been engaged to facilitate. Often it is unspoken, even publicly denied, but it becomes obvious by the actions of the organization over time.

The second is the focus on tools and techniques to remove waste (*muda* in Japanese). Organizations desperately want their people to know *how* to use the tools and techniques, but rarely invest sufficiently to ensure they understand *why* these tools and techniques exist and how they fit into a bigger business strategy.

The third is the focus on removing waste (muda) without considering overburden (*muri* in Japanese) or unevenness (*mura* in Japanese). These second two aspects are seemingly unknown to so many! This coupled with the often-unchanged organizational politics and policies means that waste is normally removed within functional silos, but overall, little benefit is seen, as waste is often only moved from one area to another. As a subset of the focus-on-waste-only misconception, there are also some who believe that speed of production should be the priority or focus.

The fourth misconception is the belief that the executive team doesn't need to be engaged in the program, the learning, and the coaching of their people. The idea that learning a new set of tools and techniques to enable the removal of waste is a frontline-worker and middle-manager thing seems pervasive throughout upper management the world over.

The fifth misconception appears in roughly half of the companies I have worked with. It is the idea that everything must "look professional." Not that I am averse to things looking professional, but it often gets in the way of actually getting things done. I call this "Pretty Lean," where the focus seems more on making things appear professional and in control; often just behind the facade is an archaic organization struggling to meet its customers' needs.

Another misconception, number six so far, is the belief that considerable amounts of bureaucracy in documenting, auditing, and otherwise employing a handful of people in the "cottage industry" of administering Lean is necessary. Measuring the organization's "Lean maturity" as if there is some level of mastery that enables an organization to stop "doing Lean" is not necessary; nor is the perceived need to employ people to collect, collate, and present reams of data.

Misconceptions seven to nine could arguably be combined into a single description, but I think they are distinct enough to list separately. Number seven is the error of discrete implementation: optimizing individual areas of a business without considering the connections and handoffs between them. Rather than optimizing the whole, the organization focuses on each individual unit, area, line, etc. They then try to maximize efficiency in each area, often at the cost of redundancy and overprocessing in supporting or connecting areas.

Number eight, and arguably a heading under which all others could sit, is the belief that Lean fits well in traditional western business practices. This does not mean that Lean is an eastern business practice, but that it is (or should be) its own business management system that should be run holistically across the organization. It is not something that fits well within principles based on command and control and short-term return on investment (ROI) where the next quarter's results sit at the top of the priority list. There is nothing wrong with ensuring positive ROI in and of itself, but the focus on getting those returns as quickly as possible limits the long-term benefits as will be discussed.

The ninth misconception, as I see it, is the idea that something that took decades to develop and continues to evolve and improve, can be learned, applied, and perfected in a matter of months. Danaher, arguably the most successful "copier" of Lean, took several years to develop and build their Danaher Business System.

The final, and I argue, the biggest, misconception with Lean as applied in most organizations is that there doesn't need to be a focus on learning. Specifically, the lack of double-loop learning seems prolific.

HEADCOUNT REDUCTION

In simplest terms, the value of Lean, the real competitive advantage, comes when an organization realizes the potential of engaging the entire workforce in the efforts to improve the organization. Too many organizations have focused their efforts on learning the tools and techniques, how to use them, and the returns they can get on the investment, their ROI. They want whatever investment they make in learning these tools and techniques to be paid back within a certain time frame, and in most organizations, this needs to be quantifiable.

How do they quantify it? In manufacturing organizations, it can come from reduction in inventories, reduction in floor space needed, reduction in defects and quality complaints, etc. But for many organizations, manufacturing included, the benefits they seek are counted in the number of people removed from the business.

There is an inherent problem when organizations work toward removing waste through the efforts of the frontline employees, with the end objective being to remove these same frontline employees. There is an inherent problem when organizations focus merely on the outputs of the system without understanding the impact of the inputs and the processing.

Every system, every action everyone takes, at any time, can be simplified into, and described as, a process. As I write, the process is simply the thinking of the words I want to write (input) and the conversion of thought to action in my fingers (processing), with the output being the words on the screen. Of course, there are other levels or processes involved: the processing of the inputs of my pressing the keys to the output of the letters and words appearing right before my eyes. We could drill down deeper to the individual 1s and 0s within the computer and the inputs that are then processed by individual circuits within the chip. Figure 1.1 is a simple process flow diagram demonstrating the above process.

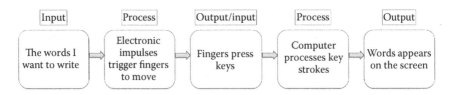

FIGURE 1.1
Basic process thinking.

The point is that everything is a process; Lean is no different, but the desired output seems to have shifted from its original intent of creating capacity to enable growth to creating capacity to enable layoffs. Of course, not all organizations are using Lean to reduce headcount. However, reduction in headcount, while sometimes necessary, should not, in any way, be associated with improving processes through the application of Lean thinking. Not unless all responsibility and efforts to improve processes sit entirely with the management, something Frederick Taylor, the often-derided founder of scientific management, espoused in his *Principles of Scientific Management* (1911).

Furthermore, if all responsibility for improving the system and processes sits with management, then the capability and capacity for improving is now limited to a handful of individuals rather than everybody. Not only is the potential reduced, but also, the implementation of improvements becomes harder, as it is not the workers themselves creating a better system, a better process. They are now being told what to do by "those who know better," hence Taylorism and why so many view Lean and Taylorism as synonyms. They're not!

It is for this reason, the thinking that managers are there to decide how best to do the job, rather than those who actually do it, that Taylorism has long since been considered anachronistic. There is significant literature on the potential for an engaged workforce. There is an entire industry working to create more engagement, and yet, in most cases, this doesn't happen, quite possibly because Taylor's view of frontline workers still remains in the executive pools of today's industry, albeit subtly.

I would argue, and will throughout this book, that the lack of engagement is also due to the focus on getting payback rather than on building capability. Zig Ziglar (2015) said, "You don't build a business—you build people—and then people build the business." This also holds true when undertaking a shift from a traditional management system (or traditional management thinking) to a Lean management system (or Lean thinking).

Even Frederick Taylor (1911) suggested that improving productivity is a joint worker-and-management effort and should not mean lower headcounts:

> The mutual confidence which should exist between a leader and his men, the enthusiasm, the feeling that they are all working for the same end and will share in the results is entirely lacking...
>
> Through this friendly cooperation, namely, through sharing equally in every day's burden, all of the great obstacles to obtaining the [required] output...in the establishment are swept away...coupled with the daily intimate shoulder-to-shoulder contact with management, entirely removes all cause for soldiering. And in a few years, under this system, the workmen have before them the object lesson of seeing that a great increase in the output per man results in giving employment to more men, instead of throwing men out of work, thus completely eradicating the fallacy that a larger output for each man will throw other men out of work (p. 9).

Notice the phrase "through sharing equally in every day's burden, all of the great obstacles to obtaining the [required] output are swept away" (his original wording was "maximum output"). Thus there is, even in Taylor's view, over a hundred years ago, the impetus for management and frontline workers to work together to remove obstacles to greater production, to greater productivity. This cannot happen if there is a threat to jobs from improved productivity. Nobody wants to help himself or herself out of a job. As the saying goes, turkeys don't vote for Christmas.

Therefore, the value of Lean, the focus of Lean, in my view, should be on the system, the processing, and developing a greater understanding of what we do, why we do it, and how we can do it better, for everyone within the organization. The focus on developing this capability is what separates Lean from other improvement techniques or methodologies. It is not just about improving the process; it is also about creating an organizational capability to improve the process. Again, even Frederick Taylor advocated collective efforts to improve, albeit with a different set of responsibilities as to who does what in the efforts.

Many times I have heard, "It is just another process improvement technique" or "It's just a tool for management to get rid of employees." I've even heard it turned into an acronym suggesting "Less Employees Are Needed." When used as such, when the focus is on removing employees and improving the bottom line in the short term, then yes, there is a problem with Lean.

When the efforts are pooled in a small team of people, who go into various areas of a business to "Lean out that area" or "Lean that process" as if it is a one-time activity, then again, the front line will be disengaged, because they are once again being treated as they were in Taylor's time. As if the best way to improve a process is by the "clever" managers (or consultants in many cases) finding the better processes. Of course, any Lean advocate should tell you that it is the workers themselves who know the best way to do the process; how likely are they to engage and assist with improving their processes if the end result is a pink slip and a visit to the job center?

TOOLS AND TECHNIQUES

Learning the tools and techniques within a Lean management system is important; however, it is not even close to sufficient to obtain the maximum benefits possible. Just as learning how to use a hammer, saw, screwdriver, and drill does not make one a carpenter, learning how to use Single-Minute Exchange of Die (SMED), *kanban* (a Lean tool based on the Japanese word roughly translated to mean chit or slip of paper), Value Stream Mapping, etc., does not make an individual or an organization Lean.

Many organizations waste extensive resources training people how to use the tools and techniques, but do not change the organizational politics and policies to support the application. These organizations often do not provide the necessary resources, including time, to apply those tools and techniques. When they do provide the resources, there are still many barriers to effective change due to organizational structures (silos) and the traditional thinking of so many in the organization. Much of this, of course, is due to a lack of understanding of the real purpose behind what you are attempting to do. Many organizations think simple: Lean = less waste. While this is true, it is like saying the TARDIS (from *Dr. Who*) is just a police telephone box.

This focus on tools and techniques has prevailed for years. Many others have written about it. It has been so prevalent that the Shingo Prize for Excellence in Manufacturing had to be changed to the Shingo Prize for Operational Excellence to incorporate nonmanufacturing businesses, but more importantly to shift from a focus on the application of tools to an analysis of the cultural shift of an organization. Robert Miller, executive director of the Shingo Prize wrote in 2013, "The difference between successful and unsuccessful efforts was always in an organization's ability to get past the tools, events, and programs and to align management systems with principles. When such alignment took place, ideal behaviors followed and perpetuated a deep culture of operational excellence."

WASTE

Anyone who has had any involvement in Lean should know about muda, the Japanese term for waste. They will probably know at least one of a handful of acronyms such as TIMWOODS, WORMPIT, DOTWIMP, DOW(N)TIME, etc., to remember the seven or eight wastes that are collectively considered muda. For those who don't know or are relatively new to Lean, I'll use TIMWOODS to clarify these wastes:

Transportation	Moving materials from one location to another
Inventory	Raw materials, components, and finished goods
Motion	People or equipment moving or walking
Waiting	For the next production step, interruptions of production
Overproduction	Producing more than is required
Overprocessing	Making products better than required; "gold plating"
Defects	Making substandard products or services
Skills	Underutilization of people's skills and talents

These acronyms are all variations on the original seven wastes as described by Taiichi Ohno, considered the father of the Toyota Production System (TPS). Additionally, some organizations include an eighth waste of underutilized skills (the N in downtime stands for nonutilized/underutilized talent).

I am always surprised by how few have heard of mura or muri. These are as, or potentially more, important than the seven (or eight) forms of muda. These other two create waste, and if you don't focus on removing unevenness and overburden, then your efforts to reduce waste will be in vain. Yes, you will be able to reduce waste to an extent, but if your processes and/or volumes are uneven, then there will naturally be overburden during peaks and waiting during troughs and a list of other forms of waste throughout your processes due to the unevenness and overburden.

Rather than focus on removing waste, Toyota, the company that in essence founded the Lean industry, focuses on creating flow by removing mura, muri, *and* muda; they consider all three as forms of waste, not just muda.

While removing or reducing waste is fundamental within Lean, I am arguing that it is too easy to ignore or skip the primary objective of creating capability. I'm not talking about getting a few experts in, or training up your leadership team but actively engaging everyone in the thinking behind what you're trying to do.

Simon Sinek (2009) said, "People don't buy what you do, they buy why you do it." That includes not just your purpose for your organization, the *why* you're in business, but also the *why* of starting down the road to becoming a Lean organization. Friedrich Nietzsche (1998) also alluded to this concept of providing a purpose, a *why*, with his quote, "If we have our own why in life, we shall get along with almost any how." Yet we seem to provide the lightest, least provocative why with the desire to remove waste. Why not provide the ability to grow and learn as your purpose?

There is an interesting concept within Lean that an organization never reaches the destination; that's why most of us in the Lean industry call it a journey, that we are practicing Lean, as opposed to being Lean. There is definitely some logic in that thinking. I would, however, challenge that there is a destination that can be reached when you embark on this journey: that of an organization where everyone is engaged and working toward perfection. Perfection cannot be achieved, and you will be on that journey forever, but you can build an organization where everyone is in that same boat and all are rowing in the same direction.

Lean provides the impetus for challenging the status quo, for seeing every process as something that can be improved. Arguably, improving processes is the easy bit; identifying waste is relatively simple as well, but it is the change of focus of every employee, on identifying waste, identifying problems, that only comes from a shift in organizational thinking. It is a shift from an organization where employees do as they're told by management to one where they are engaged in making things better, for everyone, including the shareholders.

Lean is not just a methodology to engage people, or to make it easier for them to do their jobs. This aspect makes it much easier to sell to people if they believe their jobs will become easier, but it also must come with some expectation that they will not lose their jobs as a result. When this happens, when the organization gets everyone engaged and thinking about how to do their jobs better, then the results will be far superior to those achieved when the organization is only looking to remove waste.

SPEED- OR TIME-BASED MANAGEMENT

There is also, within the Lean community, a slightly misguided drive for ever-faster products and services, or *time-based management*. This also misses the point of Lean. It is one approach that can be taken, but it doesn't apply to all organizations or industries. *Heresy*, I am hearing people say. Even in manufacturing, it is not all about faster. The basic principle of takt time establishes the right speed for production. Very few companies couldn't make their products faster than they currently do. If the demand isn't there, then there is no point in making your products faster or making more of your product. So speed, while beneficial in some cases, is not the objective. The objective is flexibility, adaptability, but not necessarily speed.

Speed is a by-product of flexibility. It is the added bonus we get when we focus on creating a capability within the organization to adapt to changes in customer demand. It is not about making the product faster or completing the service faster, but about the ability to adjust speed, up *and* down, as changes in demand require.

Even when organizations are growing, there will be products and services that begin to reduce in volume as new products replace them. The ability to adapt quickly, to change from one speed to another, from one product to another, comes from flexibility, not from being able to produce really fast. Yes, speed is a component within Lean but is not nearly as important as the ability to react to changes in demand or to changes in customer requirements. The only area in Lean where speed is crucial is in this ability to adapt and change, which only happens when everyone is engaged and understands the various mechanisms required in order to change. Thus, once again, to truly glean the full benefits of Lean, an organization needs to ensure that everyone is engaged and understands the purpose, the focus, of the management system.

EXECUTIVE ENGAGEMENT

Much has been written about the lack of engagement from executives and senior leadership. The idea that the executive team can employ a handful of experts to go in and improve an area of the business is not limited to Lean. However, when using Lean to improve your business, it is effectively putting handcuffs and an ankle bracelet on those who are making the attempt if it is merely done at the front line.

The aforementioned issues with a tools-and-techniques focus, the objectives of headcount removal, and the singular focus on removing waste are arguably due, at least in part, to a lack of understanding of both the real potential of Lean and the active role that the leadership *must* play in shifting the culture of the organization.

First and foremost, executives must understand what it is they are attempting to do when they begin their efforts to use Lean to improve their business. This sounds simple of course, and many would most likely say that they do understand. But if your understanding is aligned with any of the first three misconceptions, then I would argue that you do not truly understand what Lean is, or at least should be about: an organizational culture where everyone is engaged in making the organization better every day through learning, both individually and as an organization.

How do you get this culture? There are various views, of course. Some suggest that by starting with using the tools and techniques, the thinking of the people will change. This change will then create a change in behaviors, which will in turn create a cultural shift. There is merit in this approach, but it is not a silver bullet, not that one exists. It can be an effective approach, but I will argue that there is a simpler approach that can be used to engage everyone and create a culture of engagement that systematically solves problems, thereby creating a more effective, more efficient organization.

"PRETTY LEAN"

Although not a primary factor in the failure of Lean implementations to deliver expected results, the idea that everything should look professional is often a hindrance to speed of change and, in many cases, to engagement from the front line. In most industrial organizations, the frontline teams are focused on what works, on delivering for the business, not on what looks pretty for executives when they happen to get lost and find themselves on the shop floor. Many Lean implementations are too focused on creating visualization boards, standard work documentation, etc., that look very good but create little value.

I couldn't count the number of times I have visited an organization and seen a preprinted/fixed-layout whiteboard for managing a system that is no longer used as it was designed. They paid much more than necessary for an imprinted or laid-over grid of what they thought would be the correct items needed to manage their system only to find a few weeks or months later that they needed other information or that some of the sections were not actually necessary. They then have the problem of using something that isn't fit for purpose because they are unable to change the layout and there is no more money for replacing a poorly designed whiteboard.

Contrary to popular belief, it is incredibly unlikely that you will be able to create the perfect solution on your first pass. It is more likely that you will need to experiment with a variety of options to learn what works best with your people, your processes, and your organization and thus provides the greatest benefit.

On standardized work, Taiichi Ohno (2013) said, "Standardized work at Toyota is a framework for *kaizen* improvements. We start by adopting some kind—*any kind*—of work standards for a job. Then we tackle one improvement after another, trial and error" (p. 176; emphasis added). It should be clear by this statement that the intent is not to make pretty documents, but to make something to start with as a baseline for improvement. Your boards, systems, documents, etc., are there to be modified and improved, not to show off how much money can be spent making things look pretty.

Taiichi Ohno preferred cheap/low-cost improvements. When I worked at Toyota, I saw things such as broom heads taped to the side of a conveyor to ensure the alignment of the head unit rolling down around a curve. We used a dowel and a rag as an impromptu *andon* (a Lean tool used to call for help, based on the Japanese word for lantern). Yes, in many cases, these were temporary solutions until a more substantial, reliable, and even professional solution could be implemented. But the focus was on the functionality first and testing the solution to ensure that any money spent was spent on a proven solution. Even then, the idea that it is likely to change again should focus people's minds on keeping improvements inexpensive.

It is true that some organizations have many customer visits and the executives and sales folks want the factory floor to look good, but does the customer really think that a pretty whiteboard used incorrectly shows more control or professionalism than a dirty board used well? What would you think if you walked onto a shop floor and saw something in use, being modified and updated as the people learn how to do things better? Do we really believe that something packaged nicely actually performs any better than something that is used extensively and modified along the way? This is not your product; it is your process for creating your product. It should be flexible and adaptable, not rigid and fixed. The world changes too fast for these fixed, pretty approaches.

BUREAUCRACY

In many organizations, and arguably in many consultancy approaches, there is an overemphasis on control, something that has become the focus of management throughout the west over the last century or so. We don't trust our people to do the right thing, so we introduce all manner of control mechanisms. Sadly, when we work toward implementing Lean, we believe that this must continue.

Nakane and Hall (2002), in their article "Ohno's Method," said, "At the heart of the conflict between TPS (Toyota Production System) and orthodoxy is the managerial urge to control...Controls provide 'accountability'—called 'bureaucracy' when sign-off restrictions become onerous." In many organizations I have worked with, there is an over-reliance on bureaucracy to ensure that whatever is implemented is maintained. Even the fifth S in 5S (a method of workplace organization) is a western bureaucratic addition; when I worked in Toyota, we had only 4S; the concept of sustain was a given, and there were no audits to ensure that it happened—it just did.

Constant measurement of everything and anything that can be measured creates cottage industries within organizations that merely provide management information (MI) with the objective of control remaining a top priority for management. Rather than removing the burden of too much administrative tasking and activity for frontline managers, we seem to add more bureaucracy and administration. To get things done often requires the approval of several layers of management.

At one organization where I consulted, the internal Lean function actually wanted to set up committees within each and every function of the organization to suggest and approve changes to the methods used within the Lean program. With dozens of sites and hundreds of people, the ability to influence and affect change would have been severely hampered by the levels of bureaucracy created by the very people who should be focusing on removing bureaucracy. Fortunately, I was able to stop this before it came into play, but the fact that they had even considered it led me to believe that they didn't truly understand what they were trying to accomplish in the name of Lean.

FUNCTIONAL APPROACH

Most Lean implementations start with a single business unit or factory, and even then, sometimes only on a certain line within the factory, or a certain product or service line within a service organization. There is nothing wrong with this in principle. However, what often happens with this approach is that the organization outside of this business unit, factory, or service line has no idea what is actually going on with the Lean implementation.

This would be fine if the unit is a stand-alone entity that doesn't rely, in any way, on the other areas of the business to operate. This is a rarity, of course. Centralized purchasing, maintenance, engineering, sales, etc., are often the case, and these functions have influence on the business unit, factory, or service line. When problems arise, and they almost always do, the business unit where the implementation is underway then has to struggle with the centralized service to get them to adjust their process to suit the improving business area.

Often, this adjustment of the centralized process doesn't happen. Vested interests or uninterested managers in other areas resist the requests for changes, as these would then affect how they operate and in many cases add cost to their budget. Even worse, many of the problems that exist within business units are already known or are highlighted early on, and they involve or are even a result of processes within their supporting functions. These supporting functions are "out of scope" for the implementation, and therefore many big problems are not addressed.

The implementation team and those who work in the business unit are tasked with optimizing their processes and their performance without enabling them to make the changes necessary to truly have an impact. They then focus on what they can do, which is right given the circumstances, but it denigrates their efforts, and Lean as a whole, because people see the big problems being ignored while being asked to fix little problems within their areas. This is the opposite of what should be happening. The organization is, in effect, focusing on the trivial many, as described by Juran, and ignoring the vital few.

An aerospace organization I worked with had major problems with their supply chain and planning processes, but the organization "didn't want to know" about these problems. The focus was only on making the local function more productive. The local managers and technicians were incredibly frustrated by the effort as they were making small improvements all the while facing major challenges every day with getting parts and a decent plan for activities each day.

The concept of the support functions as suppliers to the front lines, where value is actually added, didn't take hold. Many within the organization acted as if the purpose of the business unit I was working with was to support planning or materials supply. Much of this is a result of the silo thinking and behaviors inherent within many organizations. Managers want their function to look good, even at the cost of other functions within the business. There is no high-level understanding of how they all interrelate. There is no high-level drive to optimize the entire organization, only the individual functions or lines in the profit and loss (P&L) accounts.

TRADITIONAL WESTERN MANAGEMENT PRACTICES

While many people say it is the lack of executive engagement that limits the effectiveness of most Lean adaptations, I believe there is a logical answer if we ask *why* this is the case—which means we haven't quite gotten to the root cause when we say the problem is lack of executive engagement. We have to ask why again. So why do executives not engage in the program? Why is it brought in by them but then virtually ignored on a daily basis and only measured in terms of results or ROI? Because the paradigms that exist within their mental models are not shifting. They are not opening themselves up for double-loop learning but are continuing to believe in the traditional management approach they've learned in business school, or just by operating at executive levels in the western world. These paradigms were built over decades, not as individuals but as a society, about what it takes to be successful in business both as an organization and as individuals.

Interestingly, in his book *Lean Leadership* (2000), William Lareau discusses superstitious learning. He describes how humans create beliefs based on actual events, all good so far. However, he then goes on to demonstrate that traditional business thinking, so prevalent across the globe, is based on a flawed interpretation of actual events. Of course, the United States became the dominant economic power after World War II (WWII); it was not the management practices that caused this though, but the fact that no other industrial nation had an intact infrastructure to compete against the United States. Lareau suggests that the long-held belief that the way those in the United States manage businesses created the dominance of the United States is wrong. It didn't matter what management practices were in place; the United States would have dominated regardless.

The company man learned how to get on and move up; it didn't include humility, openness to challenge, or being questioned. It was very much about command and control. The idea that the boss should have all the answers and know what to do is too pervasive for these leaders to let go and reflect on whether or not their understanding and beliefs about how to run their businesses might be flawed. It is this unwillingness or inability to shift their paradigms regarding their own knowledge and understanding of how to lead successful businesses, their unwillingness to admit that they do not have all the answers, that has held them back from truly engaging. Doing so would require admitting something that the world must never know—that they don't actually have all the answers.

The concept of double-loop learning has been around for decades. It is possible that these executives have changed or modified their underlying beliefs. They may understand that the rules of competitiveness have changed and that they not only can acknowledge they don't have all the answers but should as well. But the new paradigm regarding Lean, for most, continues to be that of an operational methodology, not an organizational learning and capability-developing system.

ROI is a great concept; I've mentioned it earlier and will again later in this book. But it is also a poor mechanism for measuring Lean activity. It is a poor mechanism for ensuring that improvements are worth the effort. Too many organizations continue to insist that any improvement must pay for itself within a given time frame. While the concept itself is not wrong, the insistence on calculating it for every improvement effort is in and of itself waste. If the organization is truly committed to improving, then any improvement should be valid.

A colleague of mine often voiced his mantra that what we want is "not a single £1,000,000 idea/improvement, but a million £1 ideas/improvements." If we all agree with this, then it should be obvious why measuring the ROI on each improvement is pure waste.

True, there are some improvements that cost a lot of money and therefore will require validation against costs, but most improvements should be done simply, cheaply. Too many organizations want to control every effort of their people; they need to feel that everything is checked and doubled-checked as to the benefit of doing it or not. In some organizations, I have even had to get confirmation that each improvement I helped with was paying itself back to the organization.

PROJECT TIMELINES

Toyota took decades to turn the thinking and activities of Taiichi Ohno into a successful business approach. Ohno started in the mid 1940s, and it wasn't until the 1970s that the changes he created started to be seen as effective enough to challenge other automakers. Danaher, as mentioned earlier, took years to develop their business system. Yet so many companies believe that they can make changes like these in a matter of months. They hire in consultants to teach them how to use the various tools and techniques and expect the changes to take hold and make incredible returns in very short time frames.

This can happen and has happened in some organizations. Several authors have written about the development of Wiremold, but even they took several years to truly see the long-term changes take hold. And Wiremold's transformation was headed directly by their CEO through his executive team, something of a rarity, I am sure. Yes, you can have bottom-line impact in a very short time frame. But if you want lasting change, cultural change, and a business-wide cultural shift, then it is going to take longer than a few months of consultants showing you how to use a handful of tools and techniques.

In most of the transformations I have been part of, the initial time frame for the project has been extended, often to double the original plan. This is not because of poor application or poor teaching, coaching, or development of people; it is because the original time frame was too optimistic. Consulting firms are notorious for underestimating how long something will take, probably because it is easier to get an extension than to win a contract in the first place.

Much of the extension work is about sustaining what has been implemented. This is necessary as people often revert to old practices whenever things get rough. However, this wouldn't be necessary if organizations were willing to invest in the long term, rather than the next quarter's financial results. The concept of ROI can be a great way of analyzing and prioritizing projects and efforts, but it can also mean necessary projects will not get full investment because the benefits in Lean implementations are indefinite, yet not always timely. Yes, we can estimate the potential improvement in the short term, but how much more will we improve once we have everyone engaged and working toward a better tomorrow each day?

Yes, there is ample evidence of what can be achieved, and often in a short time frame, but these are the exceptions, not the rule; the reasons for this are covered primarily within this chapter. If none of the aforementioned and further misconceptions are present, then yes, it is possible to make a phenomenal change to an organization in a short time frame, but this just doesn't happen often, and business leaders as well as consultants need to be more realistic with, and honest about, their expectations.

LEARNING

Throughout the rest of this book, there will be numerous references to learning—something that too many consultants and practitioners of Lean don't do and don't emphasize enough, or at all! Fundamentally, TPS is about thinking and learning. Some Toyota leaders and several consultants and academics have gone as far as to say it should have been called the "Thinking Production System" (Balle et al. 2006). Ohno, Deming, Juran, Shingo, and many others have said or at least alluded to the concept that the purpose is to get people thinking about their processes, about their systems, and challenging them.

Today's leaders don't seem to want to think about these things; they don't want to have to learn a new way of working. They want an answer to their problem that they can buy off the shelf. This doesn't exist! There is no silver bullet, no panacea for every business that can fix their problems or improve their performance. The results they seek are readily available, but it takes effort; it takes learning; it takes a shift in paradigms from what they have been taught and have learned along the way through observation of the markets.

Because it is covered in greater detail in Chapter 3, I won't go much more into learning here, but it cannot be emphasized enough. If you are not focused on learning as a primary element within your Lean implementation, then you might as well not start. If you do, please don't call it Lean; don't denigrate a great concept that has been applied poorly across the globe by or for people who don't want to think for themselves!

SUMMARY

Lean has been around for several decades. It has evolved from research into Toyota and their production system followed by the application by hundreds if not thousands of organizations and their consultants. However, many organizations, both users and "experts," have modified and adjusted the thinking to suit their immediate needs. This has created misconceptions within the industry and has, in my and others' view, denigrated the term to little more than a process improvement technique.

This evolution has in most cases reduced the potential that organizations can achieve and has sadly been used to put many thousands of people out of work. Throughout the rest of this book, I hope to demonstrate a different view of Lean and the culture desired to enable organizations not only to improve their processes and systems but also to create the capability to learn and adapt to the ever-changing world in which they operate.

In the next chapter, I will set out why organizations look to Lean to make improvements and how this influences the aforementioned misconceptions. It is not the root cause of these misconceptions, but it is, in my view, a contributing factor.

2

Why and How Companies Start Doing Continuous Improvement (CI) Activities?

According to an article by Walter Kiechel (2012) titled "The management century," we are in the third era of the "Management Century." This era, starting around 1980, includes several themes, but the focus of this book is on one, steadily improving productivity. Sure, companies would have been trying to increase productivity before 1980. There are various articles and books describing and detailing productivity improvements throughout history, and Chapter 4 covers a brief history of how and where Lean and other continuous improvement (CI) methodologies evolved. However, the past 35 years have seen dramatic increases in productivity and, of course, the drive for even more.

The nature of capitalism and competitive markets forces companies that want to stay in business to improve their productivity. To do so enables them to compete with the other players in the market. As management as a unique discipline became more prevalent and management theory, thinking, and practice became more explicit, many organizations have tried copying what has worked for others. More and more, during these last few decades, companies have turned to the latest fad to improve their organization's results.

Even where they didn't turn to the latest fad, much of traditional management thinking is based on a flawed analysis of what works, as mentioned in Chapter 1. Just because the United States became a dominant power after World War II (WWII) does not mean that the management thinking that evolved during this period was the driver. Again, as Lareau argued, virtually any management theory would have provided similar results since there was limited capability elsewhere due to the lack of intact infrastructure in the other industrialized nations at the time and thus, competition globally was negligible.

These companies hire consultants and experts in whatever is working elsewhere or whatever seems to hold the most promise. They want these experts to help them improve. Together, they copy the methods used by others in the hopes that they too can achieve the results achieved by the leaders in their industry, or in other industries where they can see similarities. This has worked to an extent in many cases, but the business world is also littered with many failed attempts at improvement. Even where efforts have provided improvement and success, in most cases, the benefits obtained were significantly less than they could have been. Also, in most cases, the benefits achieved dwindled over time as the systems and behaviors required to sustain the improvements were not in place. Had the organization approached the issue holistically and truly challenged what could be achieved, the results could have been much greater and much longer lasting.

DELAYS

Why do these attempts fail or fail to deliver as much as they could? Many reasons of course, as previously noted, but there are some underlying themes that repeat themselves over and over again. I posit that the reason companies get involved in their improvement attempt in the first place has much to do with the lack of success or at least the limited success they do achieve. In my experience, and from much anecdotal evidence given to me over the years, most companies don't start their improvement efforts until it becomes critical. As Seth Godin (2008) says, "Change almost never fails because it's too early. It almost always fails because it's too late."

Most traditionally managed companies allow problems to grow until they are forced to act, long after the ability to contain and manage the problem has passed, which means they are then playing catch-up. Whether it is declining sales, loss of market share, rising costs for a variety of reasons, or other profit pressures, they wait until the pain is unbearable, until the banks or shareholders are pressuring the executive team to cut costs "or else"!

Often this delay in reacting comes from complacency, from the feeling of comfort that comes from being dominant or at least successful in your industry for years or even decades. You may not realize you are falling further and further behind your competition until it's too late or almost too late. Even if you do realize it, you may think that your brand, your history, or your next great product is going to make things better.

In most cases, these problems start small; profits shrink mildly the first year, a bit more the second. Plans are put in place to recover, and yet the following year, the drop in profits is even worse. The executive team may have had some significant business education. The course of action chosen early on is often to make small tweaks to the budgeted figures: reductions in training, investment, innovation, recruiting, etc. Often companies get to the point where they are letting people go (in many cases, this is the first course of action). These companies are trying to manage the costs by reducing budgets and, in effect, directing people to spend less, without much instruction as to how. All the while, the profits are shrinking as smaller, more agile organizations are making great gains.

When there is a reduction in headcount or *rightsizing*, further problems arise because the amount of work rarely diminishes in correlation to the reduction in workforce. The people left feel lucky to have their jobs or are told they should, but are now faced with higher workloads and more uncertainty. Executives are notoriously bad at communicating the true picture. In many cases, you may not truly understand the full picture. You often only see the score at the end of the game. You don't see the details throughout the game that lead to the loss.

You didn't see the piles of material being sent to landfill due to poor maintenance of the equipment allowing leaks and breakdowns. You only saw the bill for materials and waste go up. You didn't realize that the savings from centralizing and reducing production planners from eight down to five meant that the local teams had to spend several additional hours each day doing localized planning. This in turn meant that those now supporting local planning are not available to actually work. Yes, the indirect labor costs have gone down, but the direct labor available has reduced as well. Unfortunately, this doesn't turn up on the quarterly results; only the reduced production or the missed customer orders do. Or possibly, you'll see an increase in direct labor costs as additional resource is brought in to cover. This signals the senior team that direct production is becoming less efficient, when in fact it has little, if anything, to do with efficiency; just poor decision making.

This lack of detailed understanding of the causes of poor performance is linked to the lack of engagement mentioned in Chapter 1. It's not that it starts when the company begins on its journey practicing Lean. Most executives do not spend much, if any time at the front line where the work is actually done. You tend to see your business from the 30,000-foot level, as detailed in spreadsheets, financial reports, and general key performance indicator (KPI) figures. You often only see the high-level problems, as demonstrated in Figure 2.1. If you were more engaged in the day-to-day operation of the business rather than merely the reporting, strategizing, and general oversight, you might have noticed the signs leading to the increased material costs, the reduced efficiency, etc.

So your executive team eventually accepts that you have to do something, but now the problems you face are much bigger than they would have been had you seen the signals and acted earlier. You failed to make the adjustments during the game; you waited until it was over; fired the coach, the quarterback, or striker who didn't score; and are now in the locker room trying to figure out what to do for next season. Except in most businesses, the next season starts tomorrow; there is no off-season.

You've allowed yourselves to believe that you were good enough, that things were good enough. That there wasn't any need to improve your operation, your business. You failed to understand that the small problems

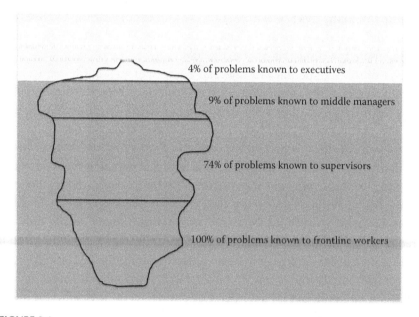

FIGURE 2.1

The iceberg of ignorance. (Adapted from McManis, L., "The Iceberg of Ignorance Debunked," http://www.thinkwaystrategies.com/iceberg-ignorance-debunked, 2016.)

seen early on were not just blips in the numbers but warning signs of things to come. You did not realize this because you do not have a culture in place that acts quickly when problems arise and digs deep to get to the root cause of the problem. You focus only on dealing with the symptoms, the results seen by your executive team in your review of overall company performance.

One of the themes that you will see further on in this book is about making problems obvious and acting on them quickly to resolve them completely. These companies that wait to act until the last possible moments are guilty of the opposite. If they were unaware of the pending troubles, then their processes and systems were not making the problems obvious. This often happens in traditional businesses where the focus on short-term goals and share price, and a lack of understanding or consideration of basic input–process–output thinking (see Chapter 1), leads executives to focus on the outcome, the result.

You may have set targets and objectives to achieve and have a plan of action to accomplish the goal but do not have the mechanisms in place to correct course when things do not go according to plan. Arguably, it is the human version of material requirements planning (MRP)—the assumption that once the plan is set, everything will go as planned and, thus, there is no need to monitor and adjust the inputs to ensure the objective is met. Helmeth von Moltke warned against this in 1892 when he wrote his treatise on military strategy. His summarized quote, "no plan survives contact with the enemy," has been used by many in reference to business as well as war (Moltke, 2009).

Interestingly, Moltke also advocated the development of subordinates to think and act on their own. He had realized that once armies (companies) grew to a certain size, the ability to command and control from the center grew weaker and weaker. Rather than setting specific instructions or orders, he provided guidance as to his intentions. Local commanders were then expected to respond to local conditions appropriately based on the guidance but also on things that he and his central team could not know about. In all likelihood, this is one of the earliest cases of empowerment where subordinates were given a framework rather than a set of specific plans to follow. Von Moltke called this Mission Command, where command was distributed to unit leaders for their specific missions.

No sports coach would ever sit in his or her office watching the scoreboard and getting upset when the other team scores. Additionally, most coaches expect their players to respond to conditions on the field and make decisions to maximize the potential for victory. Very few coaches actually demand that their players follow his or her instructions to the letter. Many executives, though, sit in their offices, reading their reports, being briefed on the status of everything. As an executive, you should be truly curious as to what is actually going on. Yet few actually make the effort to go and find out for themselves. Had you done so, you would have seen the piles of material on the floor, the operators standing waiting for the machine to be fixed or the additional staff compensating for those direct frontline people planning out the production for the day.

THE SHOW

Because it is so rare, when executives do go to the shop floor, or to their various sites, the local manager often meets them with great fanfare or at least some sort of dog-and-pony show because it is an event. If it were a routine occurrence, then there would be no need to treat it like an event, because it wouldn't be an event. So they turn up and are shown some of the problems, but the middle-level managers want to appear to be in control, so they show the executive the things they are working on to make things better.

The new piece of equipment going in, the newly promoted associate with a background in rocket science who is now in charge of reducing costs, although the person has no actual background in business, just a fancy degree from a respected university. This person will likely follow the leader's example: sit in an office, look at data on a screen, and continue to miss the inputs that are causing the results he or she is seeing. These events are often opportunities to hide the problems, especially if the local manager has any belief that he or she either is or might be held responsible for perceived failure.

The executive is shown the good things, some small but "in-control" problems that are not embarrassing for the mid-level manager, and the manager's plan for how he or she will get things back on track. The executive then returns to his or her office to contemplate his or her next bonus once that new piece of equipment kicks in and begins churning out widgets at double speed.

OK, that is an exaggeration, but the point is that far too many executives are too far removed from the day to day. They don't truly understand what goes on in their business at the front line. Problems, which could have been easily stopped and dealt with when they were small, have grown, but nobody wants to talk about them. The frontline associates have developed a work-around for all types of issues, and nobody notices and nobody cares. They do, of course, but acknowledging the issue and then doing nothing about it seems more shameful than ignoring it and then acting like you didn't know when it does get pointed out.

This level of disengagement with the front line where the work actually takes place is not limited to executives, of course. The middle-level managers also find little time to go to the shop floor, to see problems as they arise. They are often too busy reporting upward to be able see what is actually going on in their area of responsibility. Their administrative support was taken away the previous year, yet the required reports haven't been reduced; in many cases, the opposite is true. With nobody else to do it, managers spend a great deal of time actually pulling together data to present to their seniors.

I've also heard about many executives and managers and their reactions when given bad news, when told of problems: shouting, assigning blame, threats, and more. Examples provided to me were not from decades ago; this type of behavior continues in the higher echelons of business today. It's no wonder people hide problems.

This doesn't have to happen, of course, but we'll get into that as we progress through the chapters. For now, just remember the previous illustration demonstrating how organizations get into trouble by hiding or ignoring problems. In doing so, the problems become so big that the effort required to resolve them becomes gargantuan. This, in essence, creates the delay in starting down the road to fix things that are broken.

In most cases, the broken aspects of a business that is failing stem from a handful of decisions made many years ago. Like anything else, the snowball effect can be either beneficial or detrimental to success. Compound interest builds great fortunes; compound problems destroy fortunes and lives. In the examples given, decisions such as reducing maintenance costs or activity, or centralizing planning to reduce the number of planners required, would have showed positively initially, so the link to the current situation is missed.

SURVIVAL OR AMBITION?

Interestingly, when Toyota began to develop their new way of producing cars in the mid 1940s, they were in a desperate situation and at the point mentioned previously: they were in big trouble. The development of the Toyota Production System was a result of a survivalist mentality. Yet so many in the west, who are in a similar condition, rarely accept the gravity of the situation, or worse, they accept it but do not react sufficiently.

Some argue that for companies to truly engage and change their culture, they need to be in a similar condition, in survivalist mode. They talk about creating a "burning platform" to force people to change. However, there are limitations to burning platforms.

Peter Fuda (2012) discusses the psychological affect of this and suggests that instead of a burning platform that we must get off, we should focus instead on our burning ambition: what do we want to achieve? Fuda suggests that burning platforms only last for so long; a burning ambition, however, lasts until it is achieved.

Others have suggested that moving toward something good and positive is far superior to running away from something bad—when you are running from something bad, then almost anything else will do. When you are moving toward something positive, it enables focus on the goal, and the goal is clear.

Whether we stick with the burning platform or use our burning ambition, we have to then communicate that to our team. However, if we go with the burning platform, the way that this is communicated often minimizes the actual impact on the front line in terms of how they feel about the situation and the required changes. It affects their belief in the reality and criticality of the burning platform.

COMMUNICATION

This delay in starting creates a greater sense of urgency, but often only at the top of the organization. Frontline employees often don't realize how bad it is overall. They know about the problems they face in their section or division, but they do not have the overview that the executives have. In many cases, when problems are communicated from the executive team, they are either played down or exaggerated. When they are played down, the message is "we are in control" or "we have a plan," and when they are exaggerated, often the message is the same "we are in control" or "we have a plan." In either case, the front line quickly learns to interpret communications from the executives as more business mumbo jumbo, given in management speak. It becomes clear to the front line that, in general, the executives don't really know the situation, only the result. They didn't watch the game, so they only know the score. One of the things I hear over and over again is that the executive team has been saying, "We are in trouble; things are bad" many times. Often, these are efforts to exhort the workforce to "pull their bootstraps up, pull together and let's get through this!" In many cases, that is the full extent of the plan.

The more likely explanation is that the executives were aware of the problem and began attempting to communicate that things were bad. The message was received, but the actions that followed were misguided, were limited in scale or scope, and didn't achieve the necessary changes. This pattern repeats itself month after month, year after year, until the front line no longer gives any credence to the warnings from the executives that things are bad.

In many cases, those at the front line do not believe that the problem exists. They have been told many times that things were bad, that the company was in trouble, or that it needed to improve. In many cases, there is a belief that these messages are merely ploys for people to work harder.

But each time, the information indicated a need that was met without much change being seen at the front line. Or what change did occur was superficial or, the opposite, drastic. Either way, it meant the front line didn't really need to do anything—just wait for management to "do their thing" and react and adapt as best they could.

Often, this reaction and adaptation is a work-around; they find ways to cope with the decisions made by the head office. Where maintenance was reduced, the front line often acquiesces and just deals with the break-downs and leakages as they occur. Knowing in the backs of their minds that this would happen, they dejectedly muddle through each day hoping that the breakdown will happen on someone else's shift. Where planning was centralized and reduced, they accommodate by moving people around to free up the experienced people to support the planning efforts. They bring in temporary labor to cover. Not only does efficiency get worse; quality often does too.

Sadly, many of the frontline workers know what will happen as a result of the changes. They often voice their opinions on the subject. Over time, though, being ignored repeatedly, people begin to keep quiet. They know that their voices aren't truly heard, so they concede to management direction and begin to switch off that category of the eighth waste: their under-utilized brains.

WE'RE ACTUALLY DOING SOMETHING NOW, BUT IS IT THE RIGHT THING?

These companies are in trouble; they need to improve. There have been previous attempts, although in many cases, they were limited to slogans and banners imploring improvements with little to nothing behind them, or outright cuts in spending, including cuts in employees. The frontline teams are waiting around for management to actually do something, and they get another team of consultants showing up saying things are going to be different this time.

So now the company begins on a program of improvement, the latest management fad, and the focus is on one thing, and one thing only: improvement of the bottom-line results, this quarter! OK, I exaggerate again, although not in all cases. However, there is a huge focus on cutting costs and doing it quickly. The executive team needs results, and they need that ever-present return on investment (ROI). They need the team of consultants to pay for themselves and then some, and usually a big "and then some."

Consulting firms, large and small, often use the ROI principle to sell their work, because executives want to get what they pay for. They want to get two, three, four, or more times the money they invest in savings or in some cases increased revenue, although productivity improvement initiatives generally focus only on savings or cost cutting. This is another reason they often fail! The Jack Dixon (n.d.) quote comes to mind: "If you focus on results, you will never change. If you focus on change, you will get results."

Where is the long-term thinking? Why are we only thinking about the payback that can be counted? What about all those things that can't be counted? Deming (1993) very clearly stated, "It is wrong to think that if you can't measure it you can't manage it, a costly myth." He also cited Lloyd S. Nelson as saying, "The most important numbers in business are unknown and unknowable, management must however take them into account" (p. 35).

Declining sales, loss of market share, or rising costs cannot be dealt with in the short term only. They are indicative of a lack of good management; a short-term project to "fix" things will almost always make some improvements today, but once the project is over, what mechanisms exist to ensure things don't return to normal, back to the status quo, back to the state where this problem was allowed to develop in the first place?

Sometimes there is a mechanism to manage the specific problem; it may even be effective. But there are often similar problems unforeseen during the project, or in a separate area from what the project focused on, that creates the same problem somewhere else in the organization at a later date.

Productivity improvement projects should not really be projects at all, but a concerted effort to change the way the business thinks, the way it behaves, the culture of the organization, from one that deals with problems once they become unbearable to one that deals with them as they are noticed, and one that makes it easy to notice them early on.

Productivity improvement should become the norm, the practice of always finding better ways to do things, of constantly challenging the status quo in search of a better way, taking the long-term view of creating a dynamic organization that improvises, adapts, and overcomes obstacles to constantly stay in front.

This is one of the problems with these management fads that seemed to dominate the early part of this management era, changing course from one fad to the next, the latest method to make everything better in the organization. This constant changing of methods of improving creates change fatigue and disenfranchised employees and keeps middle management on the rebound from one to the next.

Overall, this approach of jumping from one issue to the next, trying one technique and then another, is a symptom of a lack of true strategic thinking and strategic planning. Strategic planning is not about setting the expected outcome and how to get there. It should be about setting the direction, providing guidance, and monitoring regularly to ensure both that progress is being made and that the direction is still viable for the organization.

THE EVER-CHANGING CI LANDSCAPE

Where do these business fads come from? Primarily from consultants, of course! Academic research hasn't always helped, but the primary factor, at least in my opinion, in the ever-changing business improvement methodology, is the fact that consultants have to sell. To keep selling the same thing that hasn't worked as expected; it must be changed or improved, or something new created. Often, these fads are the same thing rebranded or changed just enough to call it new. Sadly, there are plenty of us out there still doing the same thing we have always done—getting the same results we always have, and still blaming it on the client!

The changing fads are not necessarily driven by the consultants; those who work in a particular improvement methodology such as Lean, Six Sigma, Total Quality Management (TQM), Just in Time (JIT), etc., often stick to their method until it dies; they then learn the lingo and mantras of the replacement fad and carry on. Lean and Six Sigma are still thriving, although in many cases, they have been combined. The other two have become steps in the history of CI, but they are both part of Lean and Six Sigma. Chapter 4 will go into more detail on the history and various guises of CI. The message here, though, is that much of this is driven by consultants' need to sell work and management's need to improve businesses. Often, the latter is looking for the easiest, cheapest way to do so.

As an aside, I was discussing CI with a friend of mine who's an airline pilot. There has been little if any effort to take Lean or any other CI technique into the cockpit as far as I know. This is of course other than the checklist itself, something that came into existence as a result of incidents in early aviation history. Therefore, I believe that his view should be considered reasonably unbiased. He said that the executives want all the benefits of Lean, without the cost.

Just like dieters often want all their excess weight gone in a few days or weeks after piling on the pounds over years. Hence the low engagement, limited scope in terms of time frame of projects, etc. I would argue that this is reflective of society as a whole, but that's another book. In simplest terms, we want the results without the effort required to achieve them; we're lazy!

Yes, CI should not be limited to the client. But that improvement should be based on what is found in the engagement, at the front line, and in the results, not just during the sales meetings. It should also be based on research, on looking at the wider world of CI to see what others are doing—what works well and what doesn't. CI comes from learning and creating new knowledge. It does not come from doing the same thing over and over again and expecting better results each time. We must be learning and increasing our knowledge if we want to actually improve.

Sadly, many of my colleagues in this industry are not practicing what we preach. I actually had another consultant tell me he had been doing it the same way for 15 years. If there were strings of successful companies in his wake, then I would say, great! Sadly, there are not. Many of us learned our trade at Toyota, Nissan, Honda, etc. We learned how to run a production line efficiently; very few of us have begun thinking beyond the shop floor, to the entire organization and how all aspects are interrelated. We say we do, but in most cases, it is merely trying to match the language of the shop floor to that of the office, warehouse, or laboratory.

We still use nearly all examples from manufacturing, probably 80% of those from a handful of companies. There is little effort in exploring and experimenting with how the underlying principles fit into transactional processes: health care, continuous production processes (such as glass, chemical processing, plasterboard), etc., where there are no operators putting things together. In most cases, what I have seen and heard about is a clumsy effort to modify the tools and techniques to fit into the environment. Rather than focus on the principles and figure out what needs to be done in each specific case, we tend to rip off and duplicate what we have done elsewhere and force the organization to try to make it work.

In many cases, it is as bad as having a shopping list of tools and techniques to implement. When this happens, the consultant must figure a way to introduce 5S (workplace organization) to an office, for example. This is how we ended up with taped-out shapes of pens, pencils, erasers, staplers, etc. We went in with our solution and solved the problem that didn't exist. We were challenged a bit, but often, we as consultants behave similarly to executives. The inputs of the locals are often ignored as much by us as consultants as they are by executives. Maybe because we are paid well, often better than those within the client organization, we think we must have all the answers.

There are some great examples, of course—I don't want to give the impression that our industry is completely staid—but in the main, there seems to be limited development or innovation going on. Many of us are riding the wave created by Womack and Jones, without noticing the reef we're about to crash into. Jim Hudson, a fellow CI consultant working over in America, is working on releasing his own book on the subject. It is in line with my thinking, following Steven Spear in his analysis of Toyota and many other organizations. There are others, working hard to improve their own offering, to find new ways to help organizations create the desired long-term shift in culture.

THE DILEMMA

Arguably there is an inherent dilemma in consulting. Should we as trusted advisors stick to our guns as to the direction of the effort, ensuring it is right? Or should we do what the customer asks, even when we know it is not going to give them the desired results? Do we ask ourselves the question as to whether or not the two are different? Is it a compromise to do what the customer asks if we know it should at least get them moving in the right direction?

Some of the fads were better than others, some could have been great, and some are great still. However, in many cases, they don't get to deliver the results expected because expectations of results are often misaligned with expectations of effort required to achieve those results. First and foremost, any methodology, any off-the-shelf way of helping an organization, should be challenged as a matter of course to ensure that it is appropriate for the organization in question, and it must be based on sound principles not just "it worked in Company X."

In too many cases, the executive team is unwilling to put forth sufficient effort to actually make the change organization-wide. They thought, or worse, were told, that it would be good enough to just change the processes; better, more streamlined processes will make things better. Again, in the short term, they will. But how did they get so cumbersome and complex to begin with? What mechanism is in place to constantly evaluate those processes to ensure they are both delivering and consuming the same level of resources for the same or higher level of output?

Productivity improvement, like CI, cannot be a one-time project. It must be part of the organization: the way it thinks, the way it behaves, the culture of the organization. Executives need to think long term, beyond the next quarterly results or the annual bonus rounds. I'm not going to get into the financial compensation packages that often drive this behavior, although they still exist and often to the detriment of the long-term success of organizations.

However, it doesn't have to be this way. Leaders of organizations that have the foresight to think beyond their next bonus or quarterly report can treat their organization better. They can prepare it for the future, a future that will require constant change, constant adaptation to the ever-changing market place in which it operates. They can invest in a different culture, one that sees change as the norm, one that is constantly looking for ways to become better.

These leaders know that long-term capability is more important than current performance. Of course, as mentioned earlier, if you start too late, when current performance is on the verge of shutting you down, then that will remain the focus. Those who see their problems early enough have a much greater chance of truly benefiting from all that Lean can provide for an organization.

For those sitting at the far end of that scale, on the verge of terrible or getting close to it, there is still hope. As mentioned earlier, Lean was developed with a survivalist mentality; Toyota was on the brink of failure when it began looking at different ways to compete with the west. But the production practices we see today are merely what got them noticed back in the 1970s and 1980s. They have since moved well beyond that; they are still improving, not just their processes on the shop floor, but the way they develop cars, the way they develop people. They do this by constantly challenging themselves, by having a deep understanding of their processes, not by reflecting on the annual report and finding a new direction, initiative, or program to improve the results for next year. They have that constancy of purpose advocated by Deming.

For consultants, our job is to advise, not just to provide what is asked for. In the Lean industry, we often discuss Henry Ford's contribution. It was vast! One quote I've seen many times is pertinent here. Our job is not just to give our clients what they ask for, not if we want to actually make a difference long term. Ford is often incorrectly cited as having said, "If I had asked people what they wanted, they would have said faster horses" (Vlaskovits, 2011).

If we continue to ask executives what they want, they'll continue to say better efficiency, productivity, lower costs, etc. The reality is that they need greater flexibility, more adaptability, and a workforce that gives discretionary effort. That is what made Toyota what it is today. That is what has enabled Danaher to grow faster than Berkshire Hathaway (Pinsen, 2016). That is what will set one organization apart from another: not a better process, but a better method for improving processes.

In the next chapter, I will discuss the reason why capability is just as important as, if not more important than, results. Additionally, I'll present the idea that an organization must be in a constant state of change as well as a constant state of learning. I will explore some of the differences between Lean organizations and organizations that do Lean. There will also be some examples of some of the problems introduced by Lean and other CI methods, and those that will not be solved by what I refer to as traditional Lean.

3

Where Should We Focus?

I once worked in an electrical steel-pressing factory. We had around 35 presses that converted flat steel strips into stators and rotors for electrical motors. When I arrived, the company was in arrears with most of its customers. We were getting further and further behind with these orders each week. The problem we had was that the production planner had been on a training course learning the tools and techniques of Lean. He now seemed to understand that we should only make what the customer wanted each week, but he didn't seem to understand that there were underlying capabilities required to enable us to reduce our batch sizes to weekly demands from customers.

We had an incredibly poor capability for changing from one product to the next. We didn't have reliable machinery. The more changeovers we did, the more we fell behind. The more often the machines broke down, the more we fell behind. Our planning function was working on Lean principles, but the rest of the organization was not. We were trying—we had begun looking at improving our ability to change over quickly, but until we had that worked out, each changeover created more and more of a backlog with our customers.

After a few weeks in the company, I raised my concerns, which were also being noticed by others. I was asked to take over production planning, and I had to work *against* Lean principles for a time. We were increasing the batch sizes as much as possible while trying to balance the myriad of customers screaming for product. Within a month or so, we had created some breathing room; we had produced enough of every product to remove the special transportation required due to the backlog and the hand-to-mouth status of our output.

We were looking at our changeover processes, but there were conflicting views of how to improve them. Do we create a dedicated changeover team?

Do we modify the dies, the presses, the tooling to enable anyone to change from one product to the next? Arguably, a bit of everything was necessary. We didn't have a changeover team *per se*, but we had a team of people who prepared the dies, prepared the machines and the supporting equipment. We were still a far cry from world class, we hadn't gone through a full Single-Minute Exchange of Die (SMED) evolution, but we were making progress.

Our order book was looking better; we had reduced the backlog by over 50%. It was the first time in years (I was told) that we had been under £1 million in overdue orders. We were having record weeks in terms of tonnage, and the right stuff was being made. The place was starting to buzz with energy. And then the announcement of the site closure came. Too little, too late, I suppose. We were also on the verge of making a profit for the first time in years, held back quite possibly because with some products, the more we made, the more money we lost; we were still pricing some of our finished goods based on raw material prices from 5 years previous.

This is a small example of where the application of one or more of the tools and techniques, without a comprehensive understanding of how they all fit together and how some must be in place to enable others, can be detrimental to an organization. It's an example of looking at things in isolation without understanding the systemic influences. I also argue throughout this book that this practice also denigrates Lean as a concept. The idea of getting everyone engaged in a business methodology or philosophy is generally contingent on it being seen as something worthwhile, useful. It makes things difficult, if not impossible, when those who wield the weapons don't truly understand their use in the greater context of the entire organization because they have merely been given a set of instructions without being told that they need to think for themselves. They have been told that the organization wants people to think in terms of improving productivity, but they do not realize that improving the overall performance of an organization should supersede any improvement in their function. A deeper purpose is required to move beyond point-based improvement into system-wide improvement based on building knowledge through learning.

As previously noted, the Toyota Production System has also been called the Thinking Production System. No set of tools in the world will magically transform a business. To truly transform a business, the knowledge required includes a great understanding of how things fit together, how the various tools and techniques fit together, and how some are required as a prerequisite of others, depending on your current circumstances. Blindly applying individual tools and techniques to various aspects of your organization without a holistic view of how they all fit together is likely to create more problems than it will solve. In his input to Taiichi Ohno's *Workplace Management*, John Shook wrote, "[Ohno] would be distressed by the all too common focus of many practitioners to apply the various lean tools without linking them to deeper purpose" (Ohno, 2013, p. 164).

For me, this deeper purpose must be on long-term capability, not just some quick wins with simple tools. Even if you are in dire straits and you desperately need some quick wins, the long-term capability should still be foremost in your mind if you want any sustainable benefits. To sustain improvements, most people need to understand not just the what, but also the why. In Chapter 1, I alluded to Simon Sinek and his position regarding motivating people to engage with your vision, values, or purpose: "People don't buy what you do, they buy why you do it." This holds true in terms of engaging with people and getting them involved in what you are doing. They want to know why as much as what. Just telling them "it's better" is insufficient unless of course you continue to hold Taylor's belief that workers are too stupid to think for themselves. If this is the case, then why bother with Lean?

BY WHAT METHOD?

Deming (1982, 1993) often asked the question, "By what method?" To me this is about defining the how, not just the what. We often provide the objectives, the goals, for people and departments, as well as companies as a whole, to achieve. We provide a specific set of tools or techniques to achieve that goal, because we are focused on the next step. What we need is a deeper purpose that benefits everyone, not just the shareholders. To me this must be about building a capability to identify and deal with problems, to learn from the process, creating something not only tangible but also sustainable.

This long-term focus on building capability is at the heart of Lean, but too often, the focus is merely on the short-term benefits. Improve the output of a production line, remove the buildup of work in process (WIP), or reduce the costs associated with a particular unit, site, or function, normally operations. This, as well as the tangible nature of the tools, leads to a focus on learning how to use the various tools associated with Lean to remove cost rather than changing the thinking of those who use them. Of course, there is always some change in mindset; often, a new focus on the removal of waste becomes the new thinking. But removal of waste is only part of the objective. Too many in the industry still believe that merely removing waste is enough, that removing waste and improving flow will automatically develop into a culture of continuous improvement (CI).

A MODEL FOR IMPLEMENTATION

As part of his MBA thesis, Nigel Waring, a colleague in my industry, developed a simple model (see Figure 3.1) demonstrating the steps for a transformation to a Lean business model. It starts with the use of the tools, which changes the way of thinking of the people, which changes their behaviors, which then leads to a new culture. These changes in thinking, behaviors, and then culture are created through coaching, not just the use of the tools.

Use of tools to develop a specific thinking, which leads to an observable behavior; when a collective group's behavior is influenced, you have changed their "culture"

We should continue to use the traditional improvement tools but in a new and different way:

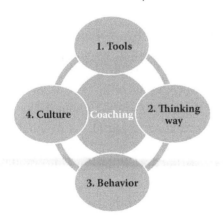

The *real* value of Lean tools

- Use the improvement tools in the daily workplace to solve real issues.
- Coach cognitive learning to create new thinking and behavior.
- Tools are unimportant; thinking and behavior are all that matter.
- This is how Toyota develop the "Thinking way" of the people.
- The tools, KPIs, and coaching are combined to create maximum synergy.

FIGURE 3.1
Summary of tools–thinking way–behaviors–culture model. KPIs, key performance indicators. (From Waring, N., "What is the difference between Toyota and the rest of the automotive world?," MBA thesis, University of Cardiff, 2005.)

On the surface, this is a very simple concept. However, there are underlying assumptions that are only true if we understand the full thinking behind the model, and even Waring warns against taking this model/image at face value. First and foremost is that the tools will achieve the desired results only if they are strategically selected and used to solve real business issues. Yes, they should, if applied correctly or, as is often not the case, selected correctly. Many tools within the Lean toolkit were developed to solve specific problems. They can be used in other organizations, but they often need to be modified to suit the specifics of those organizations; in many cases, a different tool or technique, not inherently part of the Lean toolkit, is more appropriate.

Assuming you do achieve the desired result in terms of the tool used, the next assumption is that "seeing is believing." Yes, an old adage that holds true in most cases, but just because people see something happen, they are very often biased against accepting a view different than their own. Confirmation bias often leads people to ignore the evidence in front of them if it contradicts their view of how things should be. Barker (2001) discusses this and Thomas Kuhn's work in his video on paradigms. It is the coaching and focus on how people think and the requirement for people to think differently that makes the model work.

One of the reasons organizations do not achieve the desired results, though, is that in many cases, the application of the tools and techniques is limited to small areas of the business, single business units, or even single lines within a business unit. In many cases, the tools and techniques are applied to the trivial many as opposed to the vital few. Juran's explanation of the Pareto principle suggests that far too much effort is put into dealing with the trivial many, and in many Lean implementations, that is exactly what happens. The organization limits the ability of the local teams to influence or change things outside of their area of the business, and yet it is often the wider business systems and interrelationships that cause the vital few problems.

Thus, benefits gained are within the local area, and they do make things better in many cases. However, these implementations often ignore the bigger problems that are seen and felt by the frontline in their daily lives. The problems that are due to poor interaction between functions or business units remain: problems between production and materials, between materials and purchasing, etc. People will not shift their thinking in support of Lean if it only solves small problems while leaving their biggest frustrations intact.

Even if they do, just because I think differently today than I did yesterday does not necessarily mean I will change my behavior. How many smokers are very aware of the harmful effects of smoking, yet continue to puff away? Are they truly thinking differently? Who knows? Even if they are, a change in behaviors is required, and thus it is the coaching to support this change that makes the model work. Blind application of any model does not guarantee success. We must consciously focus on changing the way people think and act if we want to create capability; you cannot just use the tools and get the results—coaching for the desired outcomes in people is required.

There are plenty of people who challenge this concept of Tools, Thinking Way, Behaviors, and Culture. The general consensus in challenges centers around whether thinking way precedes behavior change or vice versa. Either way, the model suggests using the tools to change the culture through effective coaching. It is this effective coaching that I believe is too often ignored. We have been too focused on teaching and learning tools and getting improvements, and less focused on changing how people think and act through coaching.

Thus, my criticism is on the application rather than the model. Looking deeper into the thinking behind the model and the intent, it makes sense and should create the desired effect. The focus should be on changing how people think, not blind application of tools. But as with many applications of Lean, users often skim the surface and apply what can be seen and understood easily. There is often limited thinking or deeper understanding to ensure that the tools used are strategically selected to see that they are solving real business problems vs. being used to "tick the box".

Maybe the reason there aren't many success stories is that there is limited willingness to invest in the level of coaching required to make the changes in thinking and behavior. Organizations are happy to invest in learning how to use tools, but not in the coaching necessary to change the way people think about their roles. This applies both to leadership in their role as coaches for their people and with the front line.

As a result, there are limited, if any, benefits and in many cases negative consequences with regards to the people whose problems continue to be ignored, while the business introduces what in their minds is additional but unnecessary, work. If we focused as much on developing our people to think differently, to think for themselves, as we do on making improvements, then maybe we wouldn't be having this discussion?

LEARN HOW TO DO OR LEARN HOW TO THINK?

Give a man a fish, and he eats for the day. Teach a man to fish, and he eats for a lifetime. Most people have heard of this proverb or at least the sentiment behind it. The principle is sound and is regularly applied in consulting. Clients want not only the result but also the knowledge to be able to deliver the result or similar again, and ideally over and over again. They expect to learn the thought process or the technique used to deliver the result through praxis.

This is very important in Lean consultancy. Often, the primary objective is to teach the employees of the client organization how to apply the tools and techniques of Lean. Behind this is, of course, the focus on the benefits that will come, not only during the engagement but also afterward, when the client's employees carry on practicing this newfound knowledge of how to reduce or eliminate waste and shorten the lead time between initiation and completion of whatever the specific process is within the client firm.

However, the reason why this so often fails to be sustained, the reason why this book has been written, is that this focus on the results generally means that the knowledge gained is specific, focused on removing waste only, focused on how to use or create a kanban system, for example—great knowledge, but not very useful when faced with a declining market share. Just because you reduce your inventory and make only what is needed when it is needed does not mean you are automatically going to hold market share or reverse the loss in market share. It merely means that it will cost you less in effort and therefore, you'll have a higher productivity as your market share declines, but for how long?

Going back to the proverb of fishing, in teaching the tools and techniques of Lean, in essence, the client is being taught to fish, but for a specific fish, say for a rainbow trout. Great if you live in the mountains near lots of streams, but it doesn't give you much in terms of ability to catch marlin off the coast of Florida. There is nothing wrong with catching rainbow trout in the mountains. But businesses need to be flexible, to be able catch more than one type of fish.

The world is in constant flux, the business world even more so. Volatility is ever present, and businesses spend millions on mitigating the risks of the external world. Airlines buy a year's (or more) worth of fuel at a set price to avoid paying more as prices rise. Long-term contracts and vertical integration reduce variation in input prices. Investors are told to diversify to avoid the impact of any individual asset, asset class, or industrial holding failure.

All of these activities and many more are managed by vast numbers of people in all types of organizations. Corporations have risk management departments. The insurance industry is entirely based on managing risk, for individuals and organizations. Why all of this activity to manage and mitigate risk? Because things happen, the world changes, business changes, technology changes, and what is legal and what is not legal changes; to survive, businesses need to be able to deal with these changes.

During my MBA, it was said that Lean was no longer something that could be used to differentiate one organization from another. It had become a requirement to be in business, something that every business needed to be doing if they wanted to survive but not necessarily compete with the rest of their industry. It wouldn't make you stand out from the crowd; it was just enough to keep you aligned with your competition. Again, true, if you only focus on the process improvement side of Lean.

Even Ohno warned his colleagues within Toyota against copying what others did. When people were asking what Honda and Nissan were doing in the late 1950s and early 1960s, his response was that "we have to think of even better ways." Ohno (2013) said, "Even if we could see and copy what another company was doing, if we did not change it further we would only be as good as the company we had seen" (p. 80) Sure, maybe you only want to be as good as Toyota; if you're not competing with them, then that should be enough. But since everyone else is doing it, to some extent at least, then do people really believe that just copying what others do will actually set you apart from your competition?

FOCUS ON A LEARNING CULTURE

In reality, the true benefits from Lean do not come from the specific changes you make to the processes. There will be some bottom-line benefits, some savings or released capacity that enables greater growth. The real benefit comes from the cultural shift that arises once the focus is taken off the tools and techniques, and moved to the process of improvement itself, the process where we learn how to improve, how to solve problems and to deal with this ever-changing world we live in.

I doubt many readers would suggest that McDonald's has a great culture of improvement. Yes, they have been around many years and have become an icon that indicates consistency, standards, and quality (subjective, of course, but true at least to some extent). These are core facets of any Lean organization. McDonald's is an often-cited example of what executives think is meant when we talk about standardization. The fact that you can walk into a McDonald's virtually anywhere on the planet and know that you are in a McDonald's instantly is something executives like. They think that standardization should start at the top and filter out to all levels. McDonald's has a great system for maintaining their standards, and this is why their French fries, for example, taste virtually the same no matter where you are in the world!

However, I argue that McDonald's is a poor example of a Lean organization, or at best, a decent example of a traditional Lean organization. Yes, they have standards, brilliant standardization from the executive standpoint, which of course drives economies of scale—they only have a handful of packaging sizes, for example—as well as ensuring you get a reasonably standard experience each time you visit one of their more than 36,000 restaurants, almost anywhere in the world. But their standards, their "system," as even they call it, means that the majority of the frontline workers worldwide contribute virtually nothing to the growth and improvement of the processes and products. Yes, their core employees, some 20% of those who wear the uniform, will likely be encouraged to identify and make improvements, but what about the other 80%? With an employee turnover rate (depending on source) that varies between 44% and 150%, it is not surprising that frontline engagement is limited (Dunn, 2008).

Centralized standardization also means reducing autonomy at the front line. Daniel Pink's (2009a) research on motivation shows autonomy as one of the core facets that motivate people. Centralized standardization in effect reduces motivation at the front line—further disengaging employees. The focus in any Lean organization should be on the culture, the capability of the culture and the organization to deal with, even to thrive on, change. Nassim Nicholas Taleb (2012) coined the term "antifragile" to describe an individual or organization that actually increases strength from conflict, adversity, and change.

Darwin is often misquoted as saying, "It is not the strongest of the species that survives, nor the most intelligent that survives. It is the one that is most adaptable to change." Although his book *On the Evolution of*

Species and the theory behind it strongly suggested this, it was actually paraphrased by Megginson in a speech given in 1963 to the Southwestern Social Science Association in the United States and printed later that year in a textbook. Regardless of the actual source, there are few who could argue with the truth behind the statement (Quote Investigator, 2014).

The point is this: focusing on reducing waste is great. It is to every business' advantage to reduce or minimize the amount of waste in their systems and to shorten lead times to deliver their product or service to their customer. But this will never be enough to ensure that the organization can survive or even thrive in the ever-changing world in which it operates. Often, organizations spend a significant amount of time, energy, and money trying to get people to think of ways to reduce waste, but they don't change the policies and the politics that limit what people can do. They have conflicting messages in their various policies; they say they want people to reduce waste and then when processes that are entirely wasteful are challenged, the reply is "but we need it like that to ensure nobody abuses the system," for example.

Organizations, businesses, companies, etc., need to focus on their ability, their capability, to deal with changes, to react to problems faced. Management thinking often suggests that a good strategy implemented well is sufficient. Again, this is true to an extent, but any strategy, regardless of how good it is, is only good for a certain amount of time in a certain set of conditions.

McDonald's strategy has done it well: it has grown to a fantastic size with fantastic profits, and it has become, as mentioned, an icon in many ways. However, the strategy that got it here will not necessarily keep it where it is. This is true for any organization, something so often forgotten in the world. In 2015, for the first time in 40 years, McDonald's closed more stores in the United States than it opened (Buchanan, 2015).

So what is this culture, this capability to which I refer? It has to do with change, the ability to deal with, even thrive on, change: Taleb's antifragile. How does it relate to Lean and what practitioners, advocates, and executives (those who "get it") are trying to do with their processes, to reduce waste and shorten the lead time by flowing material and information straight from one end of the process to the other? Steven Spear described it in his book *Chasing the Rabbit*, now titled *The High-Velocity Edge* (2009). He also discussed it in his *Harvard Business Review* article titled "Decoding the DNA of Toyota" (1999). This culture, this capability, is about learning through solving problems.

We all solve problems every day, right? That is what many of us are actually employed to do, solve problems. It may not be specifically in our job descriptions, but in many organizations, the people who solve problems well are promoted. Except that in many cases, they don't actually solve problems well; instead, they remove the evidence of the problem, the symptom that they were seeing. I often hear, "I've got 20 years' experience"; my standard retort is, "Really? Or is it just one year's experience repeated 20 times"? I ask this because one would think that if we had encountered these problems before—which in most cases we have—then we would have found a way to make the problem go away and never come back, not just for this week, this month, or this year, but forever!

How do we do that? Not by removing the symptom, but by removing the cause, or as what has become standard management jargon, especially in the Lean world, the *root cause*. What is worse, though, is not our inability or unwillingness to actually solve problems, but the fact that we tend to promote those who are good at firefighting, those who can remove the symptoms quickly with the biggest fanfare, so that we believe they are good people. They are, of course—they have the best intentions—but their focus on removing the symptom often comes from the fact that we tend to promote based on who removes symptoms!

Waste, in most cases, is a symptom of inadequate or poor thinking and, in some cases, a complete lack of thinking. Of course, there are many examples where technology or physical constraints force us to have waste within our processes, but much of it is merely a symptom of a lack of forethought and planning during process and/or product design.

The culture then becomes one of firefighting, removing symptoms, because that is what is rewarded in the organization. People do not want to spend the time to dig into the problem, why it happened in the first place, and remove the cause, never to arise again. Why would they? This type of activity is not rewarded, probably not even recognized. It is easy to observe firefighting; it is much more difficult to observe calm, cool, collected problem solving leading to improved processes that do not require firefighting.

As an interesting aside, another friend of mine is the chief of the Fire Service in a UK region. I recently asked him how much time and/or effort they put into firefighting compared to prevention. His response further supports my position. They spend roughly four times the effort in prevention than they do on actual firefighting. Only 5% of their time is spent responding to actual fires. They have even been identified as an exemplar to the health service that more effort and focus put on prevention will reduce the efforts needed for cure. Another old adage—an ounce of prevention is worth a pound of cure.

After many years of working within the Lean industry, I have shifted my focus from the removal of waste as the primary driver to the ability, the capability, to solve problems—not just removing the symptoms but actually solving problems, ensuring that as each problem disappears, it doesn't come back. Sure, within a production environment, the reduction of waste will enable a shorter lead time and less effort than with higher amounts of waste. Outside of production, in other areas of a business, there are benefits from removing waste, but from my perspective, there are many more ways to do that than merely opening up the Lean tool kit and applying what we've been taught. Learning from mistakes, thinking through our solutions to understand the implications, and understanding how the entire business operates as a system are essential to moving from a culture of fighting fire to one of structured problem solving with the focus on learning and building knowledge to enable better thinking.

I am sure there are readers who right now are again shouting *blasphemy* regarding the previous paragraph. I would challenge you to consider how much actual thinking and learning you do on an ongoing basis to further build your own understanding of what you are doing. I am not saying that you don't challenge and learn, although I am sure there are many who don't. What I am saying, though, is that we should always be challenging our views of what we do, how we do it, and most importantly, why we do it.

This requires reflection on an individual basis as a part of our normal routines. *Kaizen*, the Japanese word often translated as continuous improvement (literally "change for the better"), actually means more than that. According to Jun Nakamura (2016), the Japanese word for continuous improvement is *kairyo*, "something you achieve externally through material and financial investments or relying on techniques of others to solve your problems." He goes on to suggest that kaizen could be better translated as "continuous self-development."

This focus on learning requires us to engage with people, the organizations we work in, and the systems and processes we use to deliver value to our customers to fully understand the overall processes, the linkages between various people and functions, and to remove the barriers to productivity. Remove or adjust policies that hold us back from being the best, not just the waste seen in the system, but anything that gets in the way. Of course, many will say that any type of barrier to productivity can be categorized into one of the basic waste categories. On the seven types of waste, Ohno said, "...waste is not limited to seven types...So don't bother thinking about what types of waste is this? Just get on with it and do kaizen" (2013, p. 175).

As I mentioned in Chapter 1, many people that I have worked with don't discuss overburden and unevenness (as a reminder, they sit right next to waste in the enemies of flow within Toyota). This leads me to believe that there are many other things that are also being ignored. It is easy to say, "It's all about removing waste." There is much to be gained from this focus. But this focus is insufficient to truly obtain the maximum benefits in the long term.

To maximize benefits in the long term, to truly get the most out of moving to a Lean business system, requires us to be learning on a continual basis. Of course, some will also say that they do learn as they remove waste. This will be true in many, if not all, cases, but in most cases, the learning is a by-product of the removal of waste, when in fact it should be the focus. I mentioned earlier that Ohno, Deming, Juran, and others all stated that the purpose of conducting experiments to improve your operation is to enable new knowledge to be created, to enable learning. Therefore, CI must include improvement of our knowledge, our understanding, and our thinking.

Jeffrey Liker's summary of Ohno as a trainer, again from Ohno's *Workplace Management* (2013), suggested that Ohno had a few basic principles for training. One of them was that "the teacher must stay ahead of the student in learning," which means that the leadership within a Lean organization needs to be constantly learning to ensure they are able to continuously train and develop their people. Liker went on to say, "Ohno himself was an obsessive learner, always at the Gemba improving TPS and improving himself, and he saw no end point for learning" (p. 167).

Too many organizations are only focused on the improvement of the process, the improvement of the bottom line for the organization. They don't seem to understand that when we limit our learning, which happens by not focusing sufficiently on it, then we limit the amount of improvement that can take place. This is because without learning, your level of knowledge remains the same. The thinking that got us here will not keep us here.

Interestingly, Taiichi Ohno is even said to have resisted documenting the work he had done in Toyota for many years. He was concerned that by documenting it, people would stop thinking for themselves; they'd stop learning and just copy what they saw. He knew what would happen, and if he were around today, he'd probably be shaking his head in shame at what people have done in his name. The last sentence of his book called *Workplace Management,* in a section titled "Selected Sayings of Taiichi Ohno," goes like this: "You are a fool if you do as I say. You are a greater fool if you don't do as I say. You should think for yourself and come up with better ideas than mine."

CLARITY

You may be confused at this point as I have suggested both problem solving and learning as the primary focus of Lean. This is because through solving problems, we are forced to learn. We learn about our processes and how they interact with other areas of our business, our suppliers, and customers. We learn about the problem-solving process. We learn about our own individual and collective limitations, biases, capabilities, and more.

Very few people, if any, would suggest that the five whys are not fundamental to the problem-solving process, any problem-solving process. When asked how the Toyota Production System came about, Ohno (2013) said, "…as a result of the sum of, and as the application of, the behavior by Toyota people to scientifically approach matters by asking 'Why?' 5 times" (p. 176). In simpler terms, the Toyota Production System is a result of solving problems. They learned how to operate more efficiently by solving problems.

For some reason, many of us want to skip this phase and go right to copying their solutions. We want to fast-forward the development phase on the assumption that what works there will work here. It may, but as mentioned earlier, it will only be enough to be as good as others. If you truly want to change your culture and become the leader in your industry, then I suggest you need to focus on solving problems to develop a culture of learning. This will last far beyond the removal of waste in your processes.

In the next chapter, we'll take a slight detour to provide a basic understanding of the development of Lean and various other CI methodologies that have surfaced over the last few decades. I believe it is important to build knowledge and understanding. A big part of that understanding comes from knowing where things come from and how they developed. Although a short history, it should provide some context for Lean alongside other variants of CI. This is also important because some of the other variants have more appropriate problem-solving methodologies for certain organizations.

4

A Brief History of Lean

To understand what we are doing with any continuous improvement (CI) program and why this focus on learning is essential, it is worthwhile to explore the history behind it, especially with regard to Lean itself. However, any account of history, where possible, should provide sufficient breadth as well as depth. Therefore, I'll try to cover the history of Lean within the context of various other CI methodologies. Since it could arguably fill an entire book, this history of CI, and Lean in particular, should not be considered exhaustive.

INTERCHANGEABLE PARTS

Depending on whom you ask, there are various starting points for CI and the industry that now exists to support organizations in their efforts to improve. Many cite the use of interchangeable parts as the beginning of CI. While I disagree, this capability was a prerequisite to mass production and thus warrants some discussion.

Although Eli Whitney is credited by some as the first to use standardized parts, there is some debate over whether or not he actually achieved this capability before others such as Mark Brunel in England, Christopher Polhem in Sweden, or Simeon North and John Hall in the United States. Whitney was, however, instrumental in pushing the concept with the United States government and thus some credit is due him for the fact that this practice is now virtually ubiquitous in industry (Gorman, 1979).

However, even these cases ignore preindustrial examples such as the Chinese manufacturing of crossbows with interchangeable bronze trigger mechanisms in the third century BC (Li et al. 2014). The Venetian Arsenal, which was using interchangeable parts almost a thousand years ago, was churning out almost a ship a day (Snapp, 2012). Honoré Blanc, a French armorer, was making muskets with interchangeable flintlocks in the late eighteenth century (Lienhard, 1997). The others listed previously were actually latecomers to interchangeable parts.

The reason I disagree that this capability was the beginning of CI is that interchangeable parts are merely a standard upon which we can improve. They are, in effect, a solution to a problem. The learning and understanding regarding how they can enable further improvement was lacking. Had it been sufficient, then there would not have been the huge gaps between application of this concept and further improvements in production practices. In simplest terms, there was a standard. Many organizations have standards; this doesn't mean they continuously challenge them, improve them, and learn new knowledge during the process.

THE INDUSTRIAL ERA, TAYLOR, AND FORD

Regardless of the exact start, the use of interchangeable parts was one of the first practices that made mass production possible. There were many improvements in manufacturing practices throughout the eighteenth and nineteenth centuries, but almost all of these were advances in technology. The invention of steam and then combustion engines released production from reliance on nature for power generation. Toward the end of the nineteenth century, the word *efficiency* became what could be considered the first management buzzword. During this period, modern management theory was beginning to develop.

Still in the late nineteenth century, Frederick Taylor was working on his *Principles of Scientific Management*; in it, he introduced the fundamental concept of a single best way to complete a task. He was focused on time and how much work could be done in a given period. Around the same time, Frank and Lillian Gilbreth were looking at the human motion required to complete repetitive tasks. Taylor and the Gilbreths had different views of workers, and although the time and motion study is now considered a single activity, at the time, they were two completely different practices.

However, time and motion studies continue today. They are used to understand work content to enable clear delineation of the activities required to complete the task and of course how long each task takes. These time and motion studies are also used to determine the required resources: equipment, tooling, parts, and of course manpower. This was not necessarily about completing the work faster, but getting the most work out of each individual.

Taylor observed and discussed the fact that people carrying out many of the heavier, more labor-intensive tasks could produce greater volumes of output with specific methods for handling materials and set rest periods throughout the day as examples. Taylor also suggested that certain jobs required certain types of people, that each person should be assigned to the tasks for which he or she is best suited.

There were many objections to Taylor's scientific management, but most were around who should determine that single best method and how much say the worker should have. Personally, I thought the way workers were described and discussed in *The Principles of Scientific Management* was appalling. Yet it seems obvious to me that many people still regard their frontline workers the same way that Taylor did: as unintelligent, unthinking mules, hired to work only, no thinking required.

Shortly after Taylor's treatise was published, Henry Ford was developing his moving assembly line, and the modern manufacturing era began. While there were other examples of assembly lines prior to Ford, most notably the Portsmouth Block Mills in the United Kingdom, it was Ford's work that gained recognition, and he is widely considered as the father of mass manufacturing.

Although Ford's assembly line received significant attention, one could argue that the first explicit understanding of the benefits of flow was British automotive manager Frank Woollard. He wrote numerous papers and appears to have been the first to "prove that achieving flow for engineered goods in low volume production (compared to Ford in the USA) resulted in costs that were as low or lower than that which could be achieved by large-scale mass production" (Emiliani and Seymour, 2011).

JAPAN ENTERS THE SCENE

On the other side of the planet, in 1924, Sakichi Toyoda (founder of the Toyoda Power Loom Company) developed a weaving loom that would automatically stop when a warp broke. Prior to this, looms would continue operating after a warp string broke, creating unsalable material that then had to be scrapped.

To me, this is arguably the true beginning of the Toyota Production System and, in my view, the beginning of CI as a concept, at least in physical terms that can be observed. However, the industry that now exists truly took decades and many others' involvement and input to develop into what we have today.

Roll on a few decades, and there were surely some advancements but nothing spectacular enough to obtain much press. After World War II, Japan, no longer focused on developing their military capabilities, began working to improve their quality to develop their industrial capabilities. At this time, Japan was seen as a low-cost but also low-quality producer.

Already in Japan to assist with the upcoming post war census, W. E. Deming, an American engineer, statistician, and quality guru, was invited by the Union of Japanese Scientists and Engineers (JUSE), to teach them Statistical Process Control (SPC). Shortly after this began, Joseph Juran was also invited by JUSE to come to Japan and teach business leaders about quality.

The two approaches were different: Deming's focus was primarily on SPC and his view that most problems in any organization were systematic, that they were due to the decisions of leadership. Juran, on the other hand, focused on managing for quality and the behaviors needed by managers to influence quality throughout the organization. Though they sound similar, any inquiry into their respective publications shows a significant difference in approach.

During this time, Kaoru Ishikawa was a member of JUSE and worked on translating Deming and Juran's works into Japanese, as well as building on the models and methods to further develop Japanese quality. He is also the creator of the Ishikawa diagram (also known as the fishbone or cause-and-effect diagram, shown in Figure 4.1) and was instrumental in, if not solely responsible for, the development of quality circles. These quality circles were teams of frontline workers whose objective was to improve the quality of their processes and the outputs from them with the support and guidance of their supervisor or manager. Quality circles were copied in many countries, and Ishikawa wrote several books on quality.

As a result of the war and various US-imposed policies to control inflation and stabilize the Japanese economy, Toyota found itself in financial trouble. They could not retain the entire workforce and, in 1951, were forced to let 1600 people go. The founder of the motor company and first

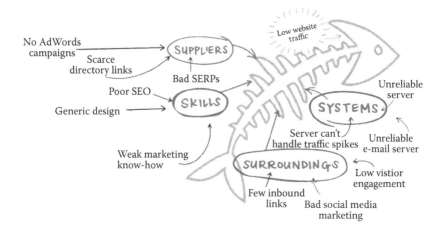

FIGURE 4.1
One of many varieties of fishbone/cause-and-effect diagrams. SEO: Search Engine Optimization; SERPs: Search Engine Result Pages.

to use the phrase Just in Time (JIT), Kiichiro Toyoda, resigned as a result. This was arguably, at least in part, due to his embarrassment over not being able to fulfill the obligation of lifetime employment that was customary in Japan and continues today. The labor issues he had faced in Toyoda Automatic Loom Works during the great depression would also have weighed on this decision.

OHNO AND SHINGO

As a result of increased orders to support the Korean War, which started shortly after this redundancy and Kiichiro's resignation, Toyota was able to remain viable and rebuild their bank balance. During this period, Taiichi Ohno was working to improve productivity in Toyota. He had started as a supervisor within Toyota in the mid 1940s after transferring from their loom works and quickly rose to more and more responsibility, possibly due to his father's relationship with Kiichiro Toyoda, the son of Sakichi Toyoda.

By the time of the restructuring of Toyota Motors, Ohno was the general manager of the Koromo Plant machining plant. When he started in this plant, he was curious about why workers only had to operate one machine. In the loom works, operators would handle up to 20 machines. This became one of the first tasks he undertook, and they began modifying machines to enable one worker to handle several machines. Shortly after Ohno started working to improve productivity in Toyota, Shigeo Shingo was brought in as a consultant to Toyota, and they worked alongside each other.

Some say Shingo did the thinking and Ohno made things happen; Shingo was said to have claimed that he was the teacher and Ohno the student; and others have asked the simple question about the chicken and the egg (Strategos Inc., n.d.). Regardless, together, they were able to change the entire production process within Toyota, focusing on flow and removing obstacles (waste) to that flow. Together, they are considered the founders of the Toyota Production System. The automatic loom invented by Sakichi sowed the seeds, but Ohno and Shingo developed the system. Their advances included the codification of the seven wastes (Ohno), Single-Minute Exchange of Die (SMED/Quick Changeover), and *poka yoke* (error proofing) (Shingo).

Arguably, the work of Deming and Juran was more focused on quality, while that of Ohno and Shingo focused on the production practices in Toyota. However, the two efforts, over time, coalesced to become the Toyota Production System, focusing on removing waste (in simplest terms).

Even this new production system was only really noticed in the west as a result of their performance during the 1973 oil crisis. As a result, GM approached Toyota, and in 1984, they agreed to begin a joint facility (New United Motor Manufacturing Inc. [NUMMI]) in California. It is likely that their quick recovery and the following joint venture prompted the 5-year study on the future of the automobile by James P. Womack, Daniel T. Jones, and Daniel Roos. The result of this research was the 1991 book *The Machine That Changed the World*, published in paperback in 2007. In this book, the term "Lean manufacturing" was first coined, potentially starting the greatest movement in performance improvement to date.

THE IN-BETWEENERS

Between this genesis of the Toyota Production System and the actual coining of the term "Lean," there were several practices that grew and then faded as they were replaced by better, more holistic approaches. JIT began gaining popularity in the 1970s and was arguably the forerunner to the Toyota Production System. However, it was conceivably a practice that would have been seen in some areas of Ford's plants as well as various other US manufacturers.

As part of the work being done to rebuild postwar Japan, the idea of doing preventative maintenance was introduced in the 1960s. By 1971, the concept of Total Productive Maintenance (TPM) with full participation of the workforce, not just the equipment technicians but operators also getting involved, was introduced by the Japanese Institute of Plant Maintenance. This TPM methodology lives on today and is the favored methodology for manufacturing organizations that rely heavily on equipment for their production, with little or no manual processing/assembly. Companies that make things like plasterboard or fiberglass often have continuous production processes that require little manual processing. The focus in TPM is to maximize production volumes by maintaining and/or improving equipment reliability.

By the late 1970s and early 1980s, Japanese manufacturing was beginning to compete well with western producers, so much so that the United States and other western countries began looking for ways to regain the lead. Total Quality Management (TQM) began in the United States as a response to this Japanese resurgence. The concept or phrase *TQM* was first coined by the US Navy in 1985 and, like JIT, lasted for a few years as a stand-alone methodology that eventually was swallowed up by Lean manufacturing in the early 1990s.

Eli Goldratt's Theory of Constraints (TOC) made its debut in 1984 in his book, *The Goal*, but this theory of improvement focused on removing the largest bottleneck (constraint), then the next largest bottleneck, and so on. Although widely practiced, it did not gain significant following. It is still practiced sporadically, but with the death of its greatest advocate, Eli Goldratt, in 2011, there is a strong chance it will fade away as others have.

Bill Smith first introduced Six Sigma in 1986 while working in Motorola in the United States. Six Sigma began as a quality program or technique and is focused primarily on reducing the variation in manufacturing and business processes. Over a few years, it grew in popularity and eventually became central to the business strategy at GE under Jack Welch. This of course would have given great kudos and attention to Six Sigma, and its popularity has grown since then. Although, arguably, it has lost ground as a stand-alone methodology, modern improvement thinking often combines it with Lean to become Lean Six Sigma or Lean Sigma.

With JIT, TQM, TPM, TOC, Six Sigma, and arguably several other lesser-known improvement movements, all emerging and providing some framework in which to improve an operation, Utah State University created the Shingo Prize for Manufacturing Excellence. Named after Shigeo Shingo, the Japanese consultant who worked with several Japanese manufacturers prior to his work in Toyota with Taiichi Ohno, the prize has come to be seen as the Nobel Prize for manufacturers.

However, over the years, the method of deciding who would or would not get the prize became tainted by the fading results of previous winners and the growing understanding that tools and techniques were insufficient to truly have a lasting impact on an organization's performance. As mentioned earlier, in 2008, the award was renamed the Shingo Prize for Operational Excellence and shifted from focusing on tools and techniques to an assessment of an organizational culture and the degree to which it reflected the Shingo Guiding Principles as opposed to the use of Lean manufacturing techniques or tools.

Business Process Reengineering (BPR) emerged at the beginning of the 1990s; interestingly, it was initiated by another Massachusetts Institute of Technology (MIT) professor, Michael Hammer, who quite possibly had discussions with Womack, Jones, or Roos, who may have introduced the concept of non-value-adding work to Hammer. He wrote an article in a 1990 issue of the *Harvard Business Review* introducing BPR, and it took off initially (Hammer, 1990). The idea that you could sit down with a small team, reengineer a process, and remove a significant amount of waste meant great returns for businesses. However, BPR was not considered a CI methodology initially; it was a one-time event. Thus, BPR became BPM, or Business Process Management, which solved the problem of the single event and made the practice more of an ongoing activity.

BPM remains today, although as it was at inception, it seems highly focused on the interaction between humans and information technology (IT) systems. Although not exclusively, enough so that it seems to be linked primarily with office-based, transactional processes where people spend the bulk of their day sitting at desks, working with computers and their associated systems.

LEAN BEGINS IN EARNEST

So now we're back in the 1990s; Lean is an emerging concept although easily understood by many as an amalgamation of the various other methodologies that had been used across industry for the last decade or two. Most people who discuss Lean think of it as a process improvement technique, akin to removing waste, creating flow, improving quality, and aligning production with customer demands.

This can be demonstrated most easily by the quote, "Lean is just another process optimization program"—something I was told in 2012 during a short discussion with a well-known UK bank CEO.

The sad thing is, in most cases, this is exactly what it is used for: to improve processes, to reduce waste, to shorten lead times. This is not wrong, in and of itself. But there is much more that it can be used for, and in reality, more it should be used for. There are some underlying principles that are too often missed or ignored by practitioners, consultants, clients, and even many academics.

This focus on tools and techniques has been so ingrained in Lean that it took the Shingo Institute 20 years to move from a tools-and-techniques measure to one that considered culture as highly as or more highly than the application of tools. If you look across the various methodologies, practices, theories, and concepts, there is a recurring theme. Fix or improve the process, and make the operation better; they are all focusing on production, at least on the face of it, definitely in the application. The primary goal, though, in all of these methodologies is to make more with less, less effort, fewer inputs, fewer defects, or all of these things.

Throughout the emergence of these improvement methodologies, the focus has been primarily on improving operations, not the entire business. Various organizations have taken the lessons inherent in the methodologies and applied them across the entire entity, but these are few and far between. In many cases, the organization will talk about an enterprise-wide system, but the evidence is again on employing the tools and techniques across the enterprise, not actually changing the way the organization works.

BEYOND THE SHOP FLOOR

In his book *The New Economics* (1993), Deming suggested that the principles he espoused, which are very much in line with and arguably lead, in part at least, to the Toyota Production System, have generally been applied only to production operations. Other areas of the business such as purchasing, finance, human resources, training, etc., had not yet seen or been part of the shift to CI.

He further suggests that thus far, organizations were missing out on approximately 97% of the potential gains that could be achieved if they moved from focusing merely on production and improving efficiency in operations by adopting what he calls the theory of transformation. Deming also said, "Anyone could be 100% successful with the 3%, and find himself out of business" (p. 37).

We need to move beyond the shop floor. We need to think about the entire organization. The focus on removing waste is applicable anywhere, but the tools and techniques that are integral to Lean do not readily translate into office-based work. It is true that they can be adapted and modified to fit office-based work. Many books on the subject have been published. Few organizations have been successful in the transition. Even those that are committed to changing how they operate often continue to focus on office work as if it were a factory floor.

One of the biggest issues with this is that reducing the lead time of an office process frequently ignores the fact that office workers normally have multiple tasks or processes that they are responsible for. They have to balance a variety of tasks, and attempting to coordinate and organize these tasks as would an operator handling several machines normally produces more frustration and angst than improvement.

To move beyond the shop floor and into the realms of the entire organization, in my view, requires a new approach, a new focus, as delineated in the previous chapter. In the next chapter, I'll set out this new approach, based on Steven Spear's *The High-Velocity Edge* and the four principles or capabilities he suggested. In the next chapter, I'll delineate the foundation for what I call dynamic organizations.

5

Dynamic Organizations

Chapter 3 provided the foundations to the idea that organizations must focus on learning to truly maximize the benefits they seek from Lean. In his 2009 book titled *The High-Velocity Edge*, Steven Spear expounded on what he had learned by researching Toyota and written about in his *Harvard Business Review* articles "Decoding the DNA of Toyota" and "Learning to lead at Toyota." In this book, he also examined aspects of Alcoa, the National Aeronautics and Space Administration (NASA), the US Navy, Southwest Airlines, and several other organizations.

The underlying premise of the book can be simplified into what he called the four capabilities of high-velocity organizations:

- Building systems and processes that make problems obvious
- Swarming to solve problems and build new knowledge
- Sharing that new knowledge gained broadly across the organization
- Leadership's role of developing these first three capabilities throughout their teams

Spear suggested many times throughout the book that it was the ability to learn and adapt that separated high-velocity organizations from the rest. Hayes, Wheelright, and Clark also wrote about learning organizations in their 1988 book *Dynamic Manufacturing: Creating the Learning Organization*, and Peter Senge, in his 1990 book titled *The Fifth Discipline: The Art and Practice of the Learning Organization* discussed the need for organizations to not just integrate, but to prioritize learning to create success.

The taken-as-true, yet incorrectly attributed, Charles Darwin quote, "It is not the strongest of the species that survives, nor the most intelligent that survives. It is the one that is most adaptable to change," further demonstrates this need for learning, both as individuals and as organizations.

The point of all this, and something that many people seem to know and understand yet struggle to practice, is that it is the ability to learn and adapt that creates survivors and, more importantly, the leaders in this world. As we discovered in Chapter 2 too many organizations attempt to incorporate Lean thinking or the practice of using Lean tools and techniques in their organizations by merely copying what others have done. These organizations attempt to learn from others, which, although admirable, means they fail to understand that it is their own ability to learn that is fundamental to their success, not their ability to copy others.

They take this cookie-cutter approach attempting to cut and paste tools, techniques, and even systems from other organizations with the mistaken belief that this will provide the same results. Sadly, the results that they seek are within their grasp. They just need to switch their focus from copying and learning simple tools and techniques, to following the principles that others have used and apply them with the required effort to learn the underlying principles of why these methods are effective. They need to create learning opportunities and to enable people to learn more about their own systems and processes.

I am continually surprised and yet disappointed by the number of managers I take out to their own shop floors, whether a factory, a bank back office, or a call center, to find they truly have little idea about what actually happens on a day-to-day basis. Yes, they understand the basic processes, they know what is done and by whom, but they don't know the detail, and they definitely don't understand the linkages between the various processes and where these linkages break down.

I also find myself continually saddened by the fact that so few leaders actually desire to learn, to build on their knowledge, in any way. Many senior managers have told my colleagues or me that they are "too old" to learn anything more. The 500-year-old adage about teaching old dogs new tricks is entirely wrong. There are plenty of people with plenty of years behind them that are out there, learning new things, new tricks, new concepts, and new knowledge every day.

Philosopher Eric Hoffer (1973) said, "In a time of drastic change it is the learners who inherit the future. The learned usually find themselves equipped to live in a world that no longer exists." How many articles and books have been written discussing the volatile, uncertain, complex, and ambiguous (VUCA) world in which we live today? I've yet to meet anyone who believes that the world we live in is stable, in any way. Yet so few people seem to incorporate learning as part of their everyday activity. So many people seem content to hold steady while the world moves forward.

Even in business school, a place where learning should be first and foremost, I remember many other students frustrated by the way we were being taught. They were expecting the straightforward lecture and note-taking. These people were ill equipped to learn for themselves; they were expecting the knowledge they believed they had paid for to be presented to them rather than having to work for it, to put the effort forth to learn for themselves. Just like the business leaders who don't actually want to learn something for themselves, these students wanted someone to hand the knowledge to them on a platter.

It is this learning, or more, the capability and the focus on learning, that separates successful, market-leading organizations from the rest of the pack. It is not the tools and techniques they use, nor the structure with which they organize functions and processes or even the caliber of the people they hire, that truly separates them from others. It is simply their focus on learning as a part of the everyday process that makes them different.

If we accept that learning is paramount, that it must be one of the core capabilities, if not *the* core capability, of an organization to be successful, then we need to have a mechanism, or a method for learning. In Chapter 1, I suggested that one of the fundamental reasons behind so many failures to maximize the potential benefits of adapting the principles of Lean was the inability or unwillingness to change the paradigms with which we see the world. I stand by this position, and throughout the following section, I plan to demonstrate how the various tools and techniques that so many have copied can be used for organizational learning, not just improving actual process efficiency.

Most people believe that it is a culture change that is needed to be truly successful with Lean. This is true in part, but it is the openness, the willingness, and the desire to learn that truly provide the greatest competitive advantage. An organization will not gain significantly more benefits merely by changing the culture and thinking to one that focuses on removing waste; it is the focus on learning that makes the difference for the organization. Therefore, the new culture must be one that prioritizes learning over merely improving processes and reducing waste.

TOOL FOCUS

When I worked in a Tier 0 supplier to Vauxhall Motors in Ellesmere Port, UK, part of GM's European arm, we had virtually all the tools and techniques practiced within Toyota—most automotive companies were reasonably quick to adopt these practices. We hadn't even come close to Toyota's low levels of inventory, but we were doing "all the right things" if you believe what many in this industry preach. Standardized work, kanbans, poka yokes, practical problem solving, etc., were ubiquitous in both our organization and Vauxhall's.

What was missing, though, as in so many other organizations, was the desire to learn. At this point, and this was in the first decade of the new millennium, some 12 or 13 years after Lean had been introduced to the west by Womack, Jones, and Roos, the focus was still on using the tools and techniques.

The western businesses that were working on their own business systems in an effort to catch up with Toyota and other Japanese manufacturers were still basing their efforts on their old paradigms of command and control; of "boss knows best." The problem solving was only really about stopping the problems—obvious enough. There was no apparent or underlying desire to learn and build new knowledge about what we were doing. Many of the beliefs inherent to traditional mass production remained, even though they were incompatible with the system we were attempting to operate under.

We had all the right practices in place, but they were superficial: taken at face value and applied rigorously, but only at the surface. It looked good to the untrained eye; even those who had been working with companies like Toyota (including myself at the time) thought we were heading in the right direction because we thought we were doing the right things. We didn't consider that doing the right things didn't make a big difference if we were doing them for the wrong reasons or didn't understand the right reasons. It didn't matter that the true benefits of the things we were doing would only become apparent if we let go of old mental models and paradigms and grasped onto something new—the idea that we didn't really know much about how our businesses actually operated.

LEARNING FOCUS

So we need to shift this thinking of Lean as a set of tools and techniques, done at the front line to optimize processes and remove waste. We need to adjust our understanding of what the culture should look like in a Lean organization. It's not just one where everyone is contributing to the removal of waste, where people are focused on improving their area's performance. It is a culture of exploration, of experimentation, with the focus on learning from everything that happens, good and bad, right and wrong—the idea that we should reflect on experiences and challenges to learn from them, not just the obvious lessons inherent in removing a problem but the factors that allowed the problem to arise in the first place. What aspect of our process design did we get wrong? Why did we get it wrong? Our paradigms for everything must be challenged on a continual basis. Even as I write this book, my paradigm for the primary theme has shifted as I realize that it is much deeper than I previously believed.

No, I am not perfect, far from it, but the requirements for creating this book include challenging my own beliefs, my own paradigms and mental models. Each time I challenge myself, they shift, not dramatically, not from yes to no, but from blue to azure, from red to rosy. Each new chapter, each paragraph, challenges what I previously thought, and this comes from being open to, no, actively looking for, new knowledge and new learning.

It is this desire to learn and improve, to challenge previously held beliefs, being open to the idea that they may have been wrong, that *we* were wrong, that is required. How do we do that? Sadly I can't force anyone to change their beliefs, but I can offer a mechanism to assist people along the way if they so desire. It is nothing new; I am not bringing anything especially new to the table here, just a different way of looking at the problem, a different way of approaching what we all do every day. Imagine an organization where every day, everyone within the organization is focused not just on removing waste or improving performance but also on gaining new knowledge to increase both the capability of the organization and the understanding of what it takes to succeed and to take the lead within their industry.

So what is this way? It includes many elements of what most people understand as Lean, but with the focus on learning, not waste, on building capability, not improving performance. The removal of waste and the improved performance will come; they are absolutely part of this approach, but they will in effect become the additional benefits rather than the focus. The focus must be on learning. Juran (1964) wrote that "whether finding new knowledge is *incidental* to one's job, or *is the job itself*, makes quite a difference. In the former case, there is no priority for acquiring new knowledge...In contrast, when one's career stands or falls on the acquisition of new knowledge, the human faculties respond with admirable vigor" (p. 59).

We must take what we know and use it to create new knowledge. This new knowledge is built or acquired through accidental discovery, systematic observation and analysis, experimentation, or importation (Juran, 1964, p. 56). The first, accidental discovery, is too random to be reliable; the last assumes sufficient similarity. The focus should be on observation and analysis and/or experimentation, which in effect is focused and planned observation and analysis. It happens from experiences and reflection on the circumstances around those experiences. So we must look at each aspect of our business, of our organization, and observe, analyze, and then reflect.

Looking at processes sounds easy, and it is, if we merely do it at the superficial level. But to gain the level of knowledge and understanding necessary, we must dig deeper into the processes, to understand them down to the minute details. Still easy to do, but there needs to be some form of prioritization to assist us; otherwise, we could be gaining great knowledge about processes that are working well while ignoring broken or misaligned processes. We should be using the problems that we face each day as opportunities to dig deep into the processes where they occur to understand how that problem came to be. Did we design the process well? Did we consider all possible outcomes? Did we create a process that makes it painfully obvious when things are not working well? Does our process make problems obvious, quickly? Or do our processes allow problems to fester and grow until they become too large to be dealt with simply, by those closest to them?

Do we reward those who solve problems when they are small and therefore are in some semblance of control at most times? Or do we reward those who, with great fanfare, "solve" the problems that have grown beyond their simple, small-impact beginnings so that everyone is aware of them because they are creating huge impacts on the business? Do we reward those who bring problems to the surface to be solved or those who hide them in the hopes that they will magically resolve themselves?

Most traditional, mass manufacturing methods focus on the latter, the hiding of problems until they become unbearable. In fact, most traditional business thinking does this; it's not just a manufacturing thing. Traditional western management culture seems to look on those who have problems as inferior to those who don't. This means people do not want their problems to be known. So we hide them. We tell our frontline workers to solve the problem, but we don't teach them how. If we do, we only worry about the solution; there is very little, if any, concern over what was learned as a result. Yes, we capture "lessons learned" after many projects and activities, but do we actually use them?

We speak the language of problem solvers, we've escalated the concept in many words across industry, with catchphrases such as "problems are opportunities," but in so many cases, the behaviors of the people within the organization demonstrate that this desire to highlight and solve problems early is not truly what is important to an organization. In many cases, the opposite is true. We talk the talk but do not walk the walk. So now I offer a different way of thinking about Lean and how it can be used to support Spear's four capabilities, what I call the elements of a dynamic organization.

Remember, the four capabilities are not a set of rules or tools to follow. There will be no prescriptions that, if followed, will automatically provide you with the desired results. This takes work, hard work, but if you focus on the principles as opposed to the application others have made, then you will set yourself on the path to knowledge. The remainder of this book will provide some guidance as to how the tools and techniques within Lean, that so many are familiar with, align with these four capabilities.

THE FOUR CAPABILITIES

Making Problems Obvious

These capabilities start with system design. How well do your systems and processes highlight when there is a problem? Or have you built your processes and the systems that support them to ensure that all problems are hidden with mountains of inventory? Problems are often hidden by a lack of clear expectations or standards with regard to the output of each process. Is there ambiguity regarding what happens before or after your process? These questions need to be answered, and answered clearly, to begin the process of making problems obvious.

In some organizations, problems don't exist, because to have a problem, we need something to compare the actual condition or results against. It may feel like a problem to some, but not to others, so no problem exists in the minds of many, and thus, nothing gets done. Defining expectations for output whether in terms of volume, quality, design, time, etc., enables unambiguous problems to exist early on. Even better is to define the expectations for inputs, processing, and outputs; this covers all aspects of any process. There is no question about whether or not something is a problem if we have defined an expectation and that expectation is not met. If we haven't defined it, then there is opportunity for discussion, debate, and further delay until we know for sure that it is a problem. All this delay allows problems to grow.

Additionally, having set clear expectations, our systems and processes need to highlight these problems as quickly as possible. Through visualization, standardization, audible warnings, physical restrictions or limitations, and various other means, we need to ensure that any deviation from our expectations is made instantly obvious to anyone and everyone nearby. The faster we can highlight problems, the faster they can be dealt with. Many of the tools and techniques within the Lean tool kit were, at least to some extent, tools for highlighting problems. Many, though, still haven't grasped that linkage. They see the obvious impact of a tool such as 5S providing a safe working environment where an operator has everything they need to do the job at hand, but 5S is as much, if not more, about highlighting problems as it is about making it easier for the operator to work.

Solving Problems

When we do finally acknowledge that a problem exists, how do we solve it? Do we truly solve it? Do we remove the root cause of the problem to ensure that it never comes back? Or do we merely remove the symptoms so that it looks good again, for now, until it happens again and we once again have to do something to remove the symptoms, because we are continually firefighting and not truly problem solving?

What method are we using to solve problems? Is it widely used throughout our organization, or do we let everyone use their own techniques hoping that at least some of them will be successful? I would argue that in most cases, it is the latter that I see. Leaders provide the instruction to solve the problem but are unwilling to provide, or incapable of actually providing, a systematic method that all can use, and thus learn from, broadly across the organization.

Whatever method is used, does it assist the problem solver in identifying and removing the root cause or just help them come up with solutions to remove the symptoms seen? Do we focus not just on learning about our processes when problem-solving but also on our problem-solving techniques? How often do we challenge our method? Remember, even Ohno suggested that we should be pushing beyond what he did, thinking for ourselves and coming up with our own improvements. We shouldn't just follow what our forebears did; we should be thinking and coming up with new and better ways.

Not only should we challenge our actual processes and systems, but we should also be challenging our problem-solving approach, our method for solving problems. We should experiment with various techniques to find the one or two that work best in our organization, in our industry. We will have different types of problems; do we use the same approach to solve all of them? Should we?

Sharing Knowledge

When we solve problems, do we spend the time to reflect on what we learned in the process? Do we go on to share the knowledge we gained with the wider organization? Is there a mechanism for that? Is it functional, i.e., does it actually help spread knowledge, or is it just a tick in the box? The mechanism for sharing knowledge needs to be simple yet effective. There are a variety of methods for this; does your organization have sufficient knowledge sharing?

Does your organization truly value knowledge? Are people seeking to learn from their own and others' efforts? Sharing knowledge means that things only have to be learned once and then shared with others to be applied by others. True, to a certain extent, real knowledge comes from investigating things yourself. People learn much more by doing than by hearing or being told what others have done, but there are many ways to effect knowledge transfer other than merely telling people what you learned.

None of this means we cannot copy things from others—in fact, much of this principle is about copying within the organization. It is the "learn once, apply many" principle that an old boss of mine used to talk about. But we are not talking about learning and copying from another organization. There is some merit in that, but as mentioned in Chapter 3, that will only make you as good as them, and few people are happy being as good; most want to be better, organizations even more so. Therefore, feel free to copy, "copy with pride," people say, but do not copy blindly. Take what others do; incorporate it into your thinking, into your designs, processes, and systems. But adapt it to suit your designs, processes, and systems. Adapt it for your environment, your market, industry, etc.

Whatever has been learned within your organization will be twice as valuable as anything learned elsewhere. This is because it already fits or is inherent within your processes and systems. It is not something that then has to be adapted to fit. It should already fit. The knowledge being shared is relevant at its source. And people who understand what you do and how you do it gained this knowledge firsthand.

Leadership Developing Capabilities

How well do our leaders develop people? Does your organization even believe that it is the job of leadership to develop their people? Many organizations want to hire in the talent with the experience in place. They believe that this experience is sufficient to deal with whatever problems arise and that experience will assist with controlling and maintaining the status quo. Unless your new hires come from an organization that understands the principles herein, it is unlikely that they will be offering anything new or different from what you've had previously. Yes, they may bring in new perspectives on things. A fresh pair of eyes can be invaluable when looking at your organization and its limitations. However, if you truly want a single, uniform culture across your organization where problems are made obvious through the application of various systems and processes that inherently do this; if you want an organization where problems are solved systematically, through a reasonably uniform and widespread technique applicable to your business and the types of problems you have; if you want the knowledge sharing across your entire organization to be valuable, relevant, and used by others upon sharing, then it is unlikely that you will get these things by hiring in from the outside without having this thinking already in place.

Far better to develop your people and create the culture and capabilities you want than to expect them to evolve through hiring in a handful of knowledgeable, experienced people. Joseph Juran (1964) suggested that there are two main roles for managers in an organization: maintaining the status quo through control and improving the situation through breakthrough.

Too many leaders believe that it is this control that is fundamental and at best pay lip service to the idea of breakthrough; of challenging current levels of performance and delivering greater quality, efficiency, effectiveness, customer service, etc., to the organization, and of course to the customers.

For organizations to become truly successful, to set the pace within their industry, they must move beyond control and focus on breakthrough, on improving. To do this, the leadership must focus on learning, on gaining and building upon knowledge. Knowledge, as mentioned earlier, is gained by accident, systematic observations and analysis, experimentation, or importing from others. Too many organizations are relying merely on accidents and importing from others. There are rarely rules or standards against systematic observations, analysis, or experimentation, but most organizations' culture and the behavior of the leadership are unsupportive of these mechanisms.

This must change; leaders need to develop their people to experiment, to systematically observe and analyze as part of their problem-solving process. The underlying objective of system and process design, besides the obvious aspect of delivering a quality output at the correct time for the next process or customer, is to make problems obvious. This needs to be coached and developed so that people consider this aspect in every process, in every improvement. The question "How easy will it be to identify problems?" should be asked for any new process or process improvement.

The need to share knowledge broadly, i.e., to import it from one area of an organization to another, is vastly underrated in every organization I have worked with. Even when working in Toyota, many of the leaders there were doing the right things but not necessarily coaching and developing me (or others) to understand the wider implications of why we did what we did. In fact, many people who have worked in Toyota do not actually understand this higher-level aspect of the processes, tools, and techniques in use. We learned how to do things and, in many cases, why, but rarely at the highest level of system-wide thinking and how all the various aspects supported each other. I have heard many times from previous Toyota employees, "I didn't realize what we were doing until I left."

Even Toyota hasn't fully engrained this level of focus on learning, arguably because it has become inherent, and therefore, it doesn't necessarily need to be so explicit. I would argue, though, that even Toyota would benefit from making this focus more explicit.

It was obvious from a production perspective, but from a learning perspective, it was hidden, covert, tacit knowledge that could have been more explicit, but could then potentially run afoul of Ohno's belief that people should be thinking and learning for themselves. Don't limit the thinking of people by thinking that copying is sufficient. Merely doing what others do is not enough. You must find new ways to remove waste, new ways to improve processes. Lean is a great overarching system, but at the heart of it needs to be a willingness, a desire, to not just copy what has been done elsewhere but truly develop a workforce that thinks for itself, challenging anything and everything.

SUMMARY

Throughout the rest of this book, I'll provide some basic linkages between the Lean tools and techniques and the four principles espoused by Spear. I'll simplify the principles into *see*, *solve*, *share*, and *show*. I'll demonstrate that there is nothing wrong with the tools and techniques in and of themselves, but their blind application minimizes their potential benefit. It is through understanding that learning must be included and prioritized to maximize the benefits of the tools. This means not that you must use the tools, but that if you do, then you will increase the benefit your organization obtains by switching from a focus on the tool and the impact on your process to a focus on the learning that each application can provide to incrementally shift from "as good as others," to leading the pack.

6

The Principles within Lean

No book on Lean would be complete without some discussion about the various tools. OK, not exactly true, but my intention within this book is to demonstrate that, although I believe our current methods of implementing Lean in organizations across the world are flawed, they are not a million miles from where they should be. In fact, in many cases, the foundations have been laid well, but the design of use afterward is lacking—lacking the focus on learning and building knowledge, lacking the focus on thinking, or should I say, on higher-order thinking.

Throughout the next section of the book, my aim is to discuss a variety of tools and techniques that many business leaders and most Lean practitioners and advocates should be familiar with, if not experts in. But in this final chapter of Section I, I intend to demonstrate the additional value of the tools and techniques beyond what can be seen on the shop floor and in the bottom line. I intend to demonstrate how the tools and techniques that most practitioners are familiar with and use on a daily basis have a little gem hidden within that is all too often ignored. They provide an inherent mechanism for facilitating thinking, and thus learning, within the organization.

Of course, standardized work, done correctly, will produce the best possible quality with the least amount of effort required in the shortest time. But it also provides a simple mechanism for identifying problems, an invaluable baseline for analysis when solving problems, and an organization-wide template for sharing knowledge gained from solving problems that do arise. Standardized work also provides leadership with a mechanism for coaching, through process confirmation, for guiding frontline workers through the process of creating it, and by providing an instrument to focus discussions on improvement.

There are some who say standardized work should not be thought of as the current best practice, that to do so makes it harder for people to accept that it needs to be challenged and improved. Taiichi Ohno referred to standardized work as merely a basis for improvement. Whatever terminology or phrase you associate with standardized work, it must be understood that it provides much more than just a method for accomplishing the work.

THE VALUE OF KNOWLEDGE

Not all tools that are part of the Lean tool kit fit within or support the four capabilities. Some are merely the solution for certain specific problems that crop up in many organizations across many industries. Even Toyota states that many of the tools are merely workarounds until they can find a better method of achieving the objective, whatever it is. Toyota has their concept of true north, which for them is to be able to deliver a vehicle at the end of the assembly line customized in accordance with the customer's desires, just as he or she orders it.

Yes, this true-north concept is far-fetched, an objective that will never be reached, but it is this objective that sustains the drive for continuous improvement. They are always searching for ways to get closer to that objective in the improvement efforts they make each and every day. Having a clear unambiguous goal, regardless of whether or not they can achieve it, focuses all involved on working toward it, with the understanding that no single effort, not even significant coordination of efforts across hundreds of sites with thousands of people, will make it possible in the foreseeable future.

But this clear unambiguous goal will require new knowledge to be obtained. Whatever your true-north concept is, it is unlikely that the knowledge you currently have is sufficient to achieve it, and therefore, you must build new knowledge: about yourselves, your processes, and of course your products, amongst other things. This new knowledge will not be attained through copying others; it can only be created through reflection, thinking, and gaining deeper and deeper understanding of what it is that you do.

Whatever the tool, I am arguing that while they are great for removing waste, creating better quality or at least ensuring quality, planning improvements, reducing batch sizes, etc., the real benefit comes from the learning that takes place, or that should take place from using them. We should be forcing ourselves to think and find new and unique solutions to problems, not just copy and paste what has been done elsewhere. Toyota is constantly developing their system; it is not set in stone, so it evolves. Your process improvement techniques should as well.

There is some history to this concept: Ohno is reported to have said, "Do not codify method." Deming asked, "By what method"? There have been various arguments about whether or not your improvement method should be codified. What is key with this to me is not whether or not it is codified, but whether or not it is improved; just as your production processes are improved, your method for improving should also be challenged and tweaked along the way. It is not something that should be set once and forgotten about or merely assumed fit for purpose. As discussed earlier, the world is changing, your market is changing, and therefore your business must change and adapt to stay relevant and competitive.

Consider this excerpt from Deming's *Out of the Crisis* (1982): "It is a hazard to copy. It is necessary to understand the theory of what one wishes to do or make. We are great copiers. The fact is that the Japanese learn the theory of what they wish to make, then improve on it" (pp. 128–129).

I would like to think that people would engage much more if they understood that the efforts put forth are about more than just making more money for the company, more than just removing waste and, in many cases, removing people (no, they are not the same!). We (the Lean industry) often talk about the benefits to the frontline workers: things like better ergonomics, a safer workplace, and fewer frustrations. Their frustrations are essentially forms of waste and hence should be removed or at least reduced as much as possible. But we rarely discuss the benefits of learning, possibly because so many people seem averse to the idea. Maybe the idea that we have learned everything we need at school, or that if we wanted to learn, we should go back to school, is too pervasive to overcome. I'd like to think this is not the case; however, the evidence I have seen, as well as feedback I've had from many peers, suggests that this is at least in some part true.

I've already stated that the efforts exerted in using the tools should be with a dual purpose, the first being the obvious intent with which so many people are already familiar. The second purpose is to create the conditions for new knowledge to be gained by all, with the expectation that new knowledge will become part of the routines of the people within the organization. True, not everyone wants to learn, as acknowledged previously, but this may be because of the traditional paradigm that if someone has many years of experience, it should mean they know a lot, and this just isn't always the case.

This assumption that time spent in a given activity automatically implies or correlates to knowledge about that activity is based on much truth, but with today's society, it is becoming less and less of a certainty.

Regardless of whether you believe that it is a result of ubiquitous information on just about everything or whether it is inherent in people to rely on others for information, the desire to grow and build on the knowledge gained while we're young seems to have waned over recent decades. Intelligence is no longer something to be proud of, but something to hide. We often shun those who put the work in to learn continuously; we often praise those who, by fortune or connection, create success from little or nothing, often by chance, with limited if any substance behind it. This often perpetuates the idea that we should be able to get our desired results without putting in the effort to achieve them.

Those who use knowledge provided by others often spurn those who create or build knowledge. The idiom that "those who can, do; those who can't, teach" is shameful; it denigrates those who have dedicated their lives to building and sharing knowledge with others and praises those who, in many cases, take that knowledge provided by these others and convert it into something "useful" to society. The foundations were built by those who "can't," and in most cases, they can but prefer the creation and building of knowledge to the use of it for other purposes.

HIGHER-ORDER THINKING

Arguably, the current trend away from traditional rote learning in schools is a result of society's realization that it does not promote learning; it promotes memorization. It promotes the lazy accumulation of knowledge provided by others, and the Internet perpetuates this paradigm. Don't get me wrong, I'm not suggesting we shut down the Internet or do away with some of the foundational aspects of primary education where rote learning is the best way to cover the basics: the times tables, spelling, basic sentence structure rules, etc. Beyond these basics, though, the educational system is learning that merely memorizing facts is a poor way to educate people.

Bloom's taxonomy (Armstrong, 2016) provides a great analogy for the primary theme of this entire book. An example is shown in Figure 6.1. We start with *remembering*—learning facts and figures. We follow this with *understanding*—we can interpret and explain concepts, not just details. We can then *apply* this knowledge in dealing with a variety of problems. However, this seems to be the extent to which most people are willing to go. At least when it comes to Lean, this is also as far as most organizations want to go. They believe that people remembering, understanding, and applying are sufficient. Few seem to have the desire to go beyond the application of knowledge gained into the realms of Higher-Order Thinking.

In Higher-Order Thinking, the top levels of the pyramid, we should be *analyzing* (understanding and comparing), which should enable *evaluating* (actually critiquing and challenging), which in turns leads to *creating* (building new knowledge based on the previous analysis and evaluation). Through this activity, we can then decide that the method, theory, concept, etc., can be improved upon and so we do.

Thus, memorizing the seven wastes, the various tools, and their prima facie purposes promotes nothing other than blind application, lower-order thinking. In some of the engagements I have been part of, the organization has used an assessment of knowledge for their internal Lean partners/coordinators/etc. The use of these skills matrices is not a problem, but the method of assessing people based on their ability to answer questions is. I have actually observed several organizations where an individual was given top marks as he or she had memorized the textbook answers to all the questions.

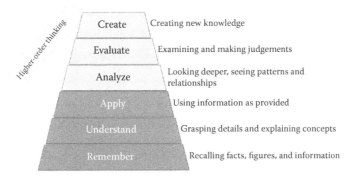

FIGURE 6.1
Bloom's taxonomy. (Adapted from Armstrong, P., Bloom's Taxonomy, Center for Teaching, https://cft.vanderbilt.edu/guides-sub-pages/blooms-taxonomy, 2016.)

I would hope that anybody reading this book will instantly see the problem with this approach, yet so many of us do exactly that. Either as external consultants or as business leaders, we've fallen into the trap of thinking that regurgitation of textbook answers proves ability. It only proves knowledge, and in this case, basic knowledge. There is no demonstration of being able to think for yourself, being able to challenge and learn to build new knowledge.

As consultants, we often go into organizations and teach the tools and techniques by rote. We get the people to follow our method, which, in some cases, hasn't changed in years. We forget, or fail to understand, the idea that continuous improvement applies to the continuous improvement method as much as it does to the production processes.

I have also handed out and seen photos of various certificates and placards awarded for completion of various training programs. Many simply state that the awardee is now competent to apply the tools (see Figure 6.2). There is no requirement that the awardees can actually think for themselves and challenge the tools or techniques, merely that they have learned how to use them, as a carpenter learns how to use a hammer. They demonstrate the lower-order thinking from Bloom's taxonomy.

When Ohno said "come up with ideas better than mine," he showed humility and leadership. He was challenging anyone who read his book to go beyond what he had done.

The entire purpose of everything we do in the name of Lean should be about building on knowledge and experimentation, not just on our

FIGURE 6.2
A graduation plaque demonstrating ability to use tools.

processes that deliver value to our customers, but also the processes we use to make our problems obvious, the processes and methods used to solve problems, and our methods of sharing the knowledge we gain along the way. We should be experimenting and finding new ways to develop our people, building knowledge and capability along the way. All of these things are just as important to challenge and improve as our production lines.

If we merely continue doing what we've done for years, someone will come along and do what I am suggesting. They will build and improve upon what we have been doing and take it to the next level. They will surpass our capabilities and create much more value than we have.

THE FOUR CAPABILITIES WITHIN LEAN

In the last chapter, I introduced the four capabilities as delineated in Steven Spear's book *The High-Velocity Edge*. These capabilities are creating systems and processes that make problems obvious, swarming to solve problems, sharing the knowledge gained from solving problems, and leadership developing their people in the first three capabilities. While I am certain these principles are sufficient for focusing efforts, they still leave the *how* question open. True, even Ohno rarely, if ever, gave instructions as to how to improve the various processes he challenged. But I would argue that we have to start somewhere, and where better than with what we already know?

I believe the four capabilities could stand alone, but I also believe it will be easier and quicker for organizations to continue using their current program and build upon it that rather than wiping the slate clean and starting over. As I mentioned at the beginning of this chapter, there are many tools within the Lean tool kit that support these four capabilities and some that don't, at least not in an obvious way. This doesn't mean we should stop using those that don't, but that we should adjust the focus, or add an additional objective, ideally a higher-order objective, when using those that do.

DEMONSTRABLE BENEFITS

Throughout the following chapters I will discuss each of the principles and provide examples and explanation of how the tools and techniques we are familiar with support them. For the remainder of this chapter, I'd like to briefly consider some examples of the application of thinking without the knowledge of specific Lean tools or techniques and how people can create significant impact on their business through solving problems and learning about how their operation works.

As mentioned previously, some of the tools and techniques within the Lean toolbox do not necessarily sit under the four principles of dynamic organizations. These tools are, in essence, solutions for specific problems inherent in many production processes. Some of them enable other tools, techniques, and principles. Several of them are, in fact, not necessarily tools or techniques, but principles in and of themselves, or at least based on principles. Examples of principles include, but are not limited to, error proofing, Single-Minute Exchange of Die (SMED), andon, etc.

These tools, techniques, or principles are worth discussing primarily because they are generally considered integral to an organization practicing Lean, but this is not always the case. The point here is that you must choose whether or not you wish to apply the principle, to what extent, and in what way, for yourself. Like the rest of the tools, they provide a baseline or foundational element of what we are trying to do, but they do not in and of themselves make problems obvious, although they can in some circumstances. They are not techniques for solving problems, although they may assist in expediting the solving of problems. And while they are not methods for sharing knowledge, in some cases, they could be used that way.

Having said all of that, there are linkages between SMED and making problems obvious. Many are familiar with the concept of "lowering the water level and exposing the rocks" as a metaphor for reducing inventory levels and exposing the problems within your systems and processes. To reduce inventory levels and produce small or single-piece batches, we must be able to move from one product variant to the next in a short time. SMED is the tool or concept we use to enable this, and thus, even SMED is an enabler of making problems obvious.

For assembly lines, this change from one product to another is often instantaneous as the products come down the production line in a mixed sequence. For some machinery, though, changing from one product to the next means changing out tooling such as stamping dies, cutter heads, forming plates, etc. The ability to move from one to the next quickly is necessary to maximize the variety of products an organization can produce in a given shift or day. This in turn enables fewer inventories to be held, but it also makes problems more obvious because any stoppage will affect the entire chain. No longer do we have piles of buffer lined up at each machine to keep it running when the upstream machines are changing product. This forces us to solve problems; otherwise, we risk shorting our customers.

There is significant literature on how to do Quick Changeover or SMED, so I won't go into detail on how to do it, only the principles behind it. The concept is fairly straightforward: you want to have your machinery operating as much as possible but with the ability to move from product to product with minimal disruption. Therefore, during a changeover, the idea is to do as much as possible beforehand to prepare for the change and leave out things that can be done afterward, for after the machine is up and running again.

Even those things that must be done while the machine is stopped should be minimized as much as possible. Switching from bolts to clamps; using alignment pins or guides to ensure the tool is set correctly as it is inserted; and having clear, well-known or documented settings to ensure that setup times are short are all aspects of this technique.

When I worked in Walkers, part of PepsiCo, we made potato chips (crisps) and a variety of other snacks. In our case, we changed from flavor to flavor, and with numerous technologies and conveyors carrying the product, the process for changing over created a variety of challenges.

We experimented with sequences for cleaning, for disassembly and washing of smaller parts, for moving from one product size to the next or one flavor to the next. After a few months of various experiments, we had reduced our changeover times from 4 hours down to less than an hour in most cases. It wasn't just about the sequencing of the changeover itself; in our case, even the production plan affected our changeovers.

Moving from certain products to other products required deeper cleans due to allergens, for example. The shelf life of the product meant that we produced every variant each week and often several times per week as the network generally only held about 3 days' stock across the United Kingdom. So we began to plan production sequences to reduce the number of full allergen cleans required each week. Starting with the basic salted variety and then moving to salt and vinegar meant we could change almost instantly. Having a second set of smaller equipment parts meant we could do the washing of certain items after production was running again.

I also spent time in a fiberglass factory; similar to plasterboard (drywall), this is a continuous process, where the product is formed or created at one end of a line and the various aspects down the line: cutting, shaping, or packaging the finished product. Often, changeovers at one end didn't affect the other. For example, changing the size of the rolls of fiberglass can be done at the packaging end of the line with no impact on the forming end. However, the nature of fiberglass production means that the processing end, the furnace and throat feeding molten glass to the spinners, stops only once every 7 years to be rebuilt.

This inability to stop processing means that any time the rest of the line is down, the factory is melting glass and spitting it out as cullet only to be fed back into the furnace for processing again: pure waste, but in this case necessary at least to some extent. The factory was very good at changing from one variant to the next, minimizing the production of cullet. They had clear specific settings for each aspect of production. They would preposition people at various key points to monitor as the change in product came down the line to switch quickly the packaging format, the size of the cut, the type of packaging even, from rolls to flat slats.

They had done all of this with, at best, limited knowledge of Lean, as had the folks in PepsiCo, at least with no official knowledge as trained from any so-called expert.

SUMMARY

The point here: it is the principle, not the specific application as presented by so many consultants, that matters. It is the idea that the organization needs to think for themselves and learn how to maximize value for their customers. Reducing the amount of waste you produce, whether that is waste in terms of product or waste in terms of effort of your staff, is the by-product of thinking and learning. These companies had solved problems without using the aforementioned tools or techniques; they had done this by thinking, by understanding their processes and the requirements of their customers, and finding the best way they could for managing both.

It is not a set of tools and techniques that did this, but a way of thinking and, of course, the act of thinking that produced better results. I would be surprised if these organizations hadn't revisited these processes and made further improvements since my tenure. Not because they have to, but because they are engaged, their people are engaged and always looking for a better way. Not because their Lean mantra says to do so, but because their leadership coaches and develops people to think and solve problems to make things better. Their leadership allows and encourages their people to experiment, to make mistakes, to learn in the process.

Section II

How the Tools Support the Learning Process

There are too many tools and techniques within Lean to cover each and every one and how they fit into or support the *see*, *solve*, *share*, and *show* principles. However, there are a few key concepts that can be demonstrated by selecting a handful of tools for each principle to demonstrate how they help make problems obvious, how they support problem solving, how they help us share knowledge, or how they enable leaders to develop their people.

In each of the following four chapters, we'll take a look at some of those key concepts and how to change the focus from using the tools because you are told to or because you merely want the obvious benefits to your bottom line to using the various tools to enable learning through problem solving.

I'll also be providing a variety of examples of how the various tools and techniques have been used in different ways to achieve similar results. This is important because I have also seen many people, primarily consultants, who act as if there is only one way to use each of the tools or techniques: that there are hard and fast rules that must be followed when implementing kanban, for example, or for how to do 5S, or for where the information center must be located and the layout that must be used. Just like the four principles, the application of the tools and techniques should be based on the underlying principle, not on "this is how I was shown to do it."

Find what works in your organization, at your location, through experimentation to enable your people to grow and develop beyond lower-order thinking and into new areas. To enable them to create experiments of their own based on new knowledge being generated everyday throughout your organization. To ensure you and your people follow the advice of Matsuo Bashō and "do not seek to follow in the footsteps of the old masters, but instead seek what these masters sought" (Ohno, 2013, p. 154).

In the appendix, I have provided a matrix of the most common tools and techniques and where they fit into each of the four principles. Most of them support multiple principles. You may disagree with some of my assertions, or quite possibly all of them. I do not write this as the expert to never be challenged. I too am building my knowledge; to a certain extent, this is an experiment to test my hypothesis. It should, however, provide a standard, a baseline to experiment against. Seek that higher-order thinking and *analyze*, *evaluate*, and *create* new knowledge.

In the next chapter, we'll look at how standardization, visualization and 5S, and *heijunka*/load leveling are mechanisms for highlighting problems as well as their inherent, well-known purposes. However, before we discuss how these tools help bring problems to the surface, we have to agree on what a problem is.

7

Making Problems Obvious

WHAT IS A PROBLEM?

It may seem obvious to make problems obvious, but history proves otherwise. Organizations and the people within them have been hiding problems probably as long as they have been in existence. There are many reasons for this: egos and overbearing bosses are a big part of it. Nobody wants to be seen or thought of as ineffective or in any way poor at his or her job. For some reason, people think that having a problem is a problem. They believe it demonstrates a lack of expertise, a lack of motivation, a lack of capability, or some other functional, character, or personality aspect that is missing. In my view, the only time when a problem demonstrates a character flaw is when it recurs, because we haven't solved it.

The fact is, we all face problems every day. Problems are what help us to grow and learn, assuming of course that we face them, solve them, and learn from them. But for decades, or centuries or even since the dawn of the human race, we've faced many, many problems; and in many groups and organizations, we've done our best to hide them. There have been a plethora of quotes, blogs, and articles over the last decade or so trying to change the language of problems; we're now supposed to call them "opportunities." Indeed a problem is an opportunity, but platitudes such as this will not help if there isn't a culture that supports this. Leaders often say things such as this and then frown on those who admit to actually having problems (read: opportunities).

This means the first thing that must be present to develop systems that make problems obvious is a true culture of acceptance of problems, almost a reverence for problems. They are, in essence, what enable us to improve. Of course we must be able to solve problems, and we'll cover that in the next chapter.

So we start with a definition of a problem, because while it may seem obvious, whenever there is more than one person involved, there is almost always a different view on events. Some may believe things are a problem, while others disagree and think things are fine. So problems, as I define them, are any deviation from the standard or the expected result. Juran (1964), in his *Managerial Breakthrough*, covered many pages discussing the various ways people interpret things differently. There are probably many other books on that subject, but the key point here is that to have a problem, we have to have some sort of expectation or standard in place.

This is quite important; In my career, I have seen many events or results raised as a problem, only to find that there was no agreed standard or expectation as to what should have been the result or what should have happened. In this circumstance, you end up with disagreement, arguments, and frustrated people, where some are trying to resolve the problem, while others do not see it as a problem and believe that the efforts being expended to solve it are wasted.

This is not necessarily wasted effort. The disagreement can force the organization to agree on the expectation. As a result of the event, they are forced to establish a standard or align expectations ensuring that any future events or activities in that realm are viewed from the same perspective.

Thus, creating a shared view of expectations, a set of standards, is essential to organizing your systems and processes to highlight problems quickly. The more we are agreed on the expectation, the easier it will be to identify when the result does not match. The more detailed our definition of the expectation, the more specific our standard, the smaller the problems need to be before they are seen and can be highlighted and resolved.

DELAYS IN PROBLEM IDENTIFICATION

This is also important. The sooner we can identify a problem, the quicker we can solve it. *And* more importantly, the sooner we see it, the smaller it will likely be. Sure, there are problems that arise that are huge at the outset, but most business problems start small and get bigger over time. The boiling frog metaphor is quite relevant here. Sure, most organizations jump out long before death (as do frogs actually), but they could have changed course much earlier, making the course change required less dramatic.

This also highlights another issue with delaying problem identification. Similar to the beer game many play in business school and in other training programs, results similar to the bullwhip effect can be seen in many business problems. Because of the delay between when the problem arises and when it is noticed and then acted upon, the actions often overcompensate for the problem, and this then requires another action to correct. This can go back and forth many times, increasing reactions to increased problems until eventually, things ease off, often due to another intervention, as those within the system are frequently unable to see the bigger picture. From this intervention, things return to a normal, controllable status. But for how long, what have we actually learned in the process?

Let's take an example of delayed problem identification. I was working with an aeroengine maintenance, repair, and overhaul (MRO) organization, and they were suffering from excessive overtime. Many organizations do. The problem they had was not one of excessive demand or insufficient capacity. They just had inadequate control over the overtime their people were working. This was primarily because the mechanism they used to manage it, reporting that was fed back from finance up to 2 weeks later, meant that by the time the management found out about the overtime, the reason it had been worked was long forgotten.

By the time they realized they were out of control, the usual actions such as a ban on overtime were ineffective because the overtime had already been worked. They were in a position that they had to do occasional overtime to manage customer expectations or deal with supply chain inefficiencies, but the extent required was not fully understood because the specific reasons why overtime was worked were known only on the day when the hours were worked. The actual hours worked, though, were not fully known to the management until at least a week later. They didn't see the cause-and-effect relationship clearly. This often happens with delayed effects.

Trying to correct the problem, reducing overtime to acceptable levels in this case, was incredibly difficult because of the delay in identifying it. They almost felt powerless to stop it because the only mechanism they had (or thought they had) was feedback from finance—true absolute figures. It took me a few weeks, but I eventually convinced them they should be looking at it daily, for the previous day. Push the decision for overtime to the frontline team leaders with the understanding of what the expectations were on a daily basis and monitor the results the next day.

We got the team leaders to report their figures daily. Sure, the numbers may not be absolutely accurate. But it didn't matter if the numbers were perfect; they had a very good idea of how much had been done, why it had been done, and were able to take the necessary actions to minimize overtime the next day. They became more proactive in dealing with overtime, because they had the information readily available. The system had been changed to highlight the problem more quickly, not weeks after the event.

STANDARDIZATION

Anyone who has ever had anything to do with any continuous improvement activity has probably heard the expression "where there is no standard, there can be no kaizen" (Ohno, 2013, p. 175). This is a direct quote from Taiichi Ohno, but Joseph Juran and W. E. Deming also suggested this in various ways in one or more of their respective books. This is in no way an exaggeration or some sort of platitude. Standards are the foundation for improvement, but they are also so much more.

How deep and detailed should the standards be? It depends! There are numerous factors to consider when introducing standards. First and foremost is why the standards are being created in the first place. Are you using this standard to replace an old standard; to improve a standard that was insufficient; to change the process due to improvements, equipment changes, legislation changes, etc.? Or just to make the expectations more clear to ensure that problems can be easily identified? Just as mentioned earlier, and supported by Ohno himself, any standard will do to begin making improvements, but we must have something on which to measure the before and after. That is the standard we start with.

Other factors to consider when determining the detail necessary in your standards include the skill level of the employees who will be using them. Are they trained, certified, or licensed individuals? If they are nurses, then they probably don't need a step-by-step instruction on how to stick a needle into an arm. If they are mechanics, then they probably don't need the details on how to turn a wrench. There are basics that all of your employees will know and plenty that they won't. There is no magic formula for developing the right level of standardization, just like there is no magic formula for developing a great process. Both of these things must be learned over time, through experimentation, through getting it wrong and learning from your mistakes.

So what is standardization? What is a standard? They come in various forms and levels of detail. One of the commonly used definitions for a standard is the "current best practice." As mentioned, there are some, of course, who think this definition is poor, as it could potentially create the belief that it doesn't need to be challenged, as it is the best practice we know. However, the reason "current" is included is because it implies that the standard can be changed, unlike the example provided in the *Business Dictionary* (BD, 2016) definition, "Written definition, limit, or rule, approved and monitored for compliance by an authoritative agency or professional or recognized body as a minimum acceptable benchmark."

A second definition provided by the Oxford Dictionary (Oxford, 2016), "Something used as a measure, norm, or model in comparative evaluations," is much closer to what we want our standards for. The comparative evaluations are what we should do with our improvement experiments to determine if they were successful in making the process better.

Unlike the width of broad-gauge railway lines, which would be incredibly difficult to change, your standards should, in most cases, be reasonably easy to change. Of course there will be some that rarely or never change. Those to do with legislation or certain technological limitations may never change. Then again, this is 2016; legislation changes almost as fast as technology, just a few years or occasionally a few decades behind the technological advances.

Another great definition or explanation of standards comes from Flinchbaugh and Carlino in their 2006 book *Hitchhiker's Guide to Lean: Lessons from the Road*. In it, they describe standards as "higher agreement." "Higher agreement, meaning the people closest to an activity or process should be in agreement about what and how an activity or process should be accomplished." They go on to discuss acceptance of this agreement: "Valuing a common way or process with low ambiguity more than you value your own way" (Flinchbaugh & Carlino's book, page 17). Both of these phrases signify that these are not dictates from central headquarters, but locally agreed methods of achieving objectives.

HOW DOES STANDARDIZATION FIT INTO SEE, SOLVE, SHARE, AND SHOW?

See

Standards provide the measure for determining whether or not we have a problem in our process. To design systems and processes to make problems obvious, we have to start with a clear expectation of the inputs, the processing, and the outputs. This standard for the process should provide sufficient detail to determine when things are not as they should be. It should also provide both frontline staff and leadership something to judge against to determine whether the process is achieving not just the outcome but any and all expectations in terms of time and effort required, quality of output, volume of output, speed of processing, etc. Nakane and Hall (2002), in their paper, "Ohno's Method," suggested that standards are the "key to process visibility."

Good standards, depending on the work, of course, even go as far as ensuring the safety of the operator, providing both the workers and management the ability to see problems that do not automatically affect the product but will affect the organization. This is not necessarily a factor in some organizations, where the risk to employees entails paper cuts and square-eye syndrome (staring at computer screens all day), but it is important nonetheless. A forward-thinking organization might have a standard that everyone takes at least two 15-minute breaks from their desk each day. For those organizations whose employees undertake physical work, whether it is assembly, repair, construction, operating equipment of many sorts, etc., the standards should clearly provide for the safety of the people.

Thus, standards should provide a mechanism to identify problems—if they're too vague then it is difficult at best to see whether or not there is a problem with the standard, the way things are done.

Solve

In terms of *solve*, standards provide the starting point for understanding what went wrong. They are the baseline in an experiment. They are the first thing that should be checked when a problem arises. Is there a standard? Is it clear? Is it sufficiently robust to ensure that this problem doesn't happen? If the answer to any of those questions is no, then the first response is likely to be to create or improve the standard.

The comparative evaluation comes into play during the analysis of the problem and in the assessment of the solution. In the analysis of a problem, we can compare the actual inputs, conditions, results, etc., to the standard, the expectation, to determine the level of deviation: how big is the problem, and where do we see it? In assessing the solution, we are ensuring that it provides a level of remedy or improvement that, at a minimum, guarantees that the standard is maintained.

Share

When it comes to *share*, standards are a fantastic mechanism for sharing the learning from solutions to problems. This may be in the form of an updated standardized work sheet, or it could be a new standard operating procedure (SOP). It all depends on what you are starting with and the necessary level of standardization for your organization and the work it does.

Obviously, or not, as I have seen, when you update a standard, it is likely that you will also need to communicate that update to anyone who is accountable to or for that standard. Part of *share* is to actually communicate with people, not just uploading all manner of information into some information technology (IT) system with the expectation that anyone who wants it will find it. I refer to Mooers' law (Mooers, 1996): "An information retrieval system will tend not to be used whenever it is more painful and troublesome for a customer to have information than for him not to have it." In this case, your employees are the customers of your information retrieval system. If it is easier not to have the knowledge than it is to find it, they will remain ignorant.

Show

It should be obvious, but in terms of *show*, it is the leaders' job to coach and develop their people to *see*, *solve*, and *share*. Much of this activity will be around standards and standardization. It is a foundational element of any improvement and thus should be one of the first principles discussed when developing people to think and learn and build new knowledge.

WHERE SHOULD STANDARDS ORIGINATE?

There will of course be a variety of reasons or requirements for your standards. Some will be corporate standards, driven by the need to keep certain administrative activities uniform across all business units. However, wherever possible, standards should be developed, written, owned, and updated by those who use them. As mentioned in Chapter 3, McDonald's is often cited as a great example of Lean, incorrectly, in my view. There is some obvious benefit to the high level of standardization across the globe, but there is also a huge drawback. If standards are universal across a global organization such as McDonald's, how is it possible for those at the front line, who often think of better ways to do things, to get their idea into the standard?

The simple answer is that it is not possible, or if it is, the effort required is huge. There are some organizations that require this level of standardization. However, I would argue that they are few and far between. The culture this creates is one of conformity, not innovation, a culture of compliance versus one of creativity. While this type of organization is usually able to introduce change across all sites quickly, it often struggles with identifying problems in the first place, and then solving problems can also be an issue, especially when it wants to update or improve the standard. In these types of organizations, both activities must be done at corporate headquarters, far from the customer and the frontline teams. The information delays discussed earlier are rampant, and thus, the problems, once recognized, are much bigger than they might have been if the local teams were empowered to manage their own business.

Additionally, centralized standards mean that solutions take a while to develop because the organization will be trying to make them perfect or as close to perfect as possible before rolling them out across the dozens or hundreds or even thousands of sites. This is necessary with corporate-wide standards; otherwise, each new update or change that comes out will potentially create new problems that will again have to go through the entire loop. The faster these loops of improvement happen, the faster we learn and improve. Forcing all improvements to go through the corporate bureaucracy virtually guarantees a sluggish pace in terms of improvement.

The delay in solving problems is a problem in and of itself. Sticking with McDonald's, it's worth noting that they have been struggling. A recent article in *Bloomberg Magazine* by Susan Berfield (2015) discussed their "system" and how difficult it was to change. They have created an organization where change is difficult and takes a long time; and while it is true that the principles of a sound process are followed in making decisions—getting facts, understanding options, moving forward in small pilot areas, etc.,—the pace of this change is phenomenally slow. According to Berfield (2015), "it took two years to develop the simple McWrap."

Too many organizations haven't learned from Helmuth Von Moltke and his understanding that attempting to control large organizations centrally was not possible. Earlier military leaders such as Napoleon and

Wellington had been able to command and control from the center, but as armies grew, this method became less viable. Von Moltke understood that it was better to give guidance and empower his subordinates to make decisions based on local conditions, things he couldn't know about from his location.

The same holds true in business. Yes, there are some universals, but not many. The principles remain true, but absolutes are a hindrance for growth, for development, for experimentation. It was Von Moltke who first said that "no plan survives first contact with the enemy." This also holds true in the corporate world, although it's not the enemy in this case, but the local conditions, the customer base, the local community, etc., that will affect the ability to implement plans as designed. In summary, wherever possible, leave the specifics to the locals. Corporate standards in general are an impediment to experimentation and thus the creation of new knowledge.

VISUALIZATION AND 5S

As an example of the aforementioned, most organizations that are on a Lean journey have some form of information center: a central area, usually on the shop floor, where they visualize the performance of the site or function within. Some organizations standardize the format for this information center. This is not terrible, but it limits the input from the people who use it. Sure, it is possible that the central function that set the standard for how this is done "knows best," but it is also possible that the local teams have great ideas for how it could be done better.

There is likely to be a conflicting message in the minds of the front line if you are asking them to experiment, to solve problems, to think, to learn, and to create new knowledge if you then follow that request with limits, especially on things they will be using very regularly. There are, of course, requirements to do this in some cases, but they should be avoided as much as possible.

Like McDonald's employees, they are unlikely to have the ability to suggest improvements, and if they do, the process to make the change, across the entire organization, is cumbersome at best. Additionally, whenever things such as this are set centrally and implemented at each site, they are often seen as another rule imposed on the locals from the central organization. Remember, change imposed is change opposed. In developing systems to make problems obvious, there is no need to dictate exactly how they must look. Provide the principle, provide examples, and go ahead and provide a starting point or baseline for them to run with, but let them develop it and modify it to suit their local conditions; the culture that currently exists will have its own nuances. Rather than dictate the exact path and destination, we should provide guidance; coach!

Visualization itself is, of course, a means for highlighting problems, but too often, our language muddies the water on this front. We talk about visualization to make it easy for anyone to know the status of the workplace. I don't want to know the status; I want to know what problems we are facing, which ones we are working on, what progress we have made. Sure, there are opportunities to demonstrate visually the connections between areas, functions, people, etc. Some of the efforts in visualization are solutions to problems such as people not knowing where to go, where things are done, or how their output fits into the bigger picture, for example.

But in the main, visualization should be an effort to bring problems to the surface, to provide transparency to ensure we cannot hide problems, from ourselves or from our organizations as a whole. It often surprises me how little this is emphasized, how little we speak about making problems obvious. There is much talk about how quickly we can see the "status." Much better, I think, to say that it provides instant identification of problems and problem areas.

Even 5S, with its many benefits, provides a simple way of identifying the problem of missing or misplaced equipment and tools. Yes, it makes the work environment safer, provides the foundation for quality work, and makes for a pleasant place to work (usually). But these could just as easily be considered secondary objectives.

Nakane and Hall (2002) wrote, "Unfortunately, when introduced in the West, 5S was often called 'housekeeping'. However, cleanliness and orderliness are only sub-goals. The main purpose of 5S is to promote process visibility, that is, to make kaizen opportunities instantly obvious." "Kaizen opportunities" could easily be read as "problems."

HEIJUNKA

The concept of *heijunka*, or leveling, is a fundamental principle within Lean that enables lower inventories and balancing out the work to manage the peaks and troughs that many organizations are faced with. Additionally, it reduces the overall lead time for each individual product or service as it enables completion of each more frequently. But in doing these things, it forces problems to the surface.

With lower inventories, we no longer have the buffers in place to cover for a machine breakdown, a parts shortage, or high levels of absence, as examples. Reducing inventories naturally makes problems more immediate when they occur, and arguably, any small glitch in your process will surface as a stoppage.

This is one of the reasons why so many organizations struggle with their attempts at Just in Time (JIT) or Lean. They see the benefits of reduced inventories in terms of lower working capital requirements and the reduced lead times for their products or services. However, they fail to recognize that in reducing inventory and running balanced production on a JIT basis, they must be very good at reacting to each and every problem as it arises. The capability to solve problems quickly and permanently is a prerequisite to running this type of operation.

Therefore, for me, we must ensure that this is as much our focus as the reduced costs, the leveled load, or the shorter lead times. We must keep the idea of finding and solving problems foremost in our minds throughout our organizations. Ignoring any problem today will inevitably mean that it is bigger, uglier, and therefore more difficult to resolve tomorrow.

Heijunka Varieties

For those who are new to Lean, heijunka or leveling is the technique used to get as close to single-piece flow as possible. It enables an organization to reduce inventories to appropriate levels based on customer demands of a day/week/month/etc. There are many books out there that explain the concept in detail, so I'll only provide a cursory look at it.

When an organization makes several products, traditional manufacturing thinking was to make economical batch sizes of each product and then switch to the next product. Lean organizations make their batch sizes as small as possible to enable inventories to be minimized. This practice, working toward, if not at, single-piece flow is leveling the load. It means that the workers need to be able to move from one product type to the next and back again many times throughout the day or week, or occasionally month, depending on the cycle times and the volumes.

When I worked at Toyota, we had three assembly lines for three different types of engines. Each assembly line had several variants. Rather than make all of one and then all of another and so on, the lines were set up to make a mix of the engine varieties throughout each shift. Traditional methods for managing this often include pigeonhole boxes, and these will be seen in the aforementioned books as the mechanism to accomplish heijunka. However, at the Toyota plant where I worked, we used three different mechanisms. One line had the traditional physical production kanbans placed onto a board to instruct the line to make that engine type. As we dispatched each engine stillage, we would pull the production Kanban from the stillage and place it onto the heijunka board instructing the line.

On another line, it was automated. There was a computer program that spread the engine variants out across the build cycle. If, as sometimes occurred, we had to stop making a certain variant due to a parts shortage or quality concern, then someone had to go into the computer program and adjust the pattern of engines coming down the line.

The third and oldest line in the factory had what we called a racetrack. It was a miniature track of conveyor, approximately 0.5 m long and maybe 30 cm wide, and it held tags in a number of positions that cycled around and around. The tags had bar codes for each engine variant, and as they passed under a scanner, that variant was sent down the actual production line. To change the sequence of engines on the line, one merely had to rearrange the tags on the racetrack.

The point here, again: it is the principle that matters, not the actual method of application. Throughout this book, one of the core principles that I am trying to get across is that each organization must figure out what works best in their circumstance, with their infrastructure, their current culture, etc. Rather than attempt to force a square peg into a round hole, find what works for you to accomplish the principle desired.

Heijunka doesn't actually work everywhere. It could, I suppose, but there are cases where it doesn't make sense. I'm sure some of my readers are again shouting *blasphemy* right now, but it's true. You don't have to level the load entirely and move to single-piece flow. I worked with a payment protection insurance (PPI) claims management company that processed hundreds of claims for their clients. Each day, they received several hundred documents from their clients and the banks with which the claims were being made.

The principle of heijunka or leveling would suggest that each document type be separated out throughout the day and phased into the workers based on takt time. There was some element of this in that they looked each morning at the volume of documents that needed processing and adjusted their workforce to suit, but otherwise, they processed the entire day's documents each day, working through all of the first type, then the second type, and so on.

One could argue that they should have leveled out the various types to be processed each day, but given that the entire processing time for each claim was somewhere in the region of 90 minutes and yet the lead times from first contact with customer to completed claim was in the region of 3 months, what would be gained? My Lean gurus reading this will suggest that there was a significant amount of waste within that lead time, and there was. However, the additional time was partly made up of waiting for the customer to complete and return documents or to speak to them to answer certain questions required by the process. The other aspect of the lead time was waiting for the banks to respond to the claims. Yes, they were working on automating certain aspects of the process to reduce the amount of time waiting for post by creating an online portal for certain aspects of the process. But the majority of the delays in the overall process were either down to the customer or the banks.

Shaving off a few minutes or even hours for document processing to be accomplished in a leveled manner throughout each day would not provide any additional benefits to either the customer or the company itself. Therefore, this solution or technique would have actually created waste rather than eliminating it.

One could, of course, argue that the processing each day was a lower level of heijunka in that each document was processed each day, but the point is, again, that if we agree that this is the case, then the application of each tool or technique is unique to the organization, and thus, it is the principle, not the specific method, that matters. Yes, they could have identified a problem earlier in the day had they set up full leveling of documents, but given the nature of the documents, there was no need for hourly interventions; daily was sufficient.

SUMMARY

Throughout this chapter I've attempted to demonstrate how a small selection of Lean tools can and should be used for making problems obvious.

In some cases, this could and should be considered their primary purpose. I've also tried to show how even with some basic concepts or principles, there are multiple methods for achieving the desired result, and therefore, it is not the "copy what I do" thinking that we should have, but more of a "show me the basic premise and I can take it from there."

We should be pushing our people to think for themselves. To do this, we need to empower them to act upon their ideas. We should be coaching them along the way: guiding them to make the right decisions and supporting them when they don't. If we don't do this last one, it won't be long before they stop.

Fundamentally, the more transparent we can make our systems and processes, the easier it will be to spot problems early. The earlier we spot them, the easier they should be to solve. Knowing that any system should make problems immediately obvious provides a requirement that is universal. How we go about doing that will depend on you, your organization, the culture, the local community, etc.

In the next chapter, I'll be looking at various methods and techniques for solving these problems that we've identified. I'll explore some of the problem-solving tools and the principles that underlie them. Again, there is more than one way to bake a cake. Find what works best for you and build on it, improve it.

8

Solving Problems

Based on the last chapter, the premise is that we would now be in a position where we are identifying problems frequently and are in need of a method to solve them. Throughout this chapter are examples of various problem-solving tools, but more important are the principles that underlie these tools. Additionally, some basic concepts are provided that many would argue are common sense, yet in many cases, not common practice.

PROBLEM-SOLVING PRINCIPLES AND CONCEPTS

Although each of the various problem-solving tools has a slightly different approach or detail and number of steps involved, they all follow a similar flow of narrowing down the problem to a single detailed problem definition to be solved, followed by root cause analysis. Root cause analysis is generally done using the Five Whys "technique," which is merely the process of asking why five times to get to the root cause. Solutions are then implemented to remove the root cause, not just the symptom.

Most of the continuous improvement (CI) methodologies, and this is definitely true of Lean, suggest that all improvements and problem-solving attempts should be treated as experiments, the smaller the better. This ensures minimal disruption to the organization and enables maximum learning with minimal risk. Thus, even when solving a problem, we should consider the process an experiment.

PDCA

Most people I've dealt with would agree that each of the problem-solving methods mentioned could be divided and then categorized into the four stages of the PDCA or PDSA cycle initially developed by Walter Shewhart, but most commonly known as the Deming cycle. PDCA stands for plan–do–check–act, and in PDSA, the word *study* replaces *check*. PDCA is as commonplace now as any other tool or technique in any improvement methodology and exists in almost all of them as a fundamental concept, not just for problem solving but also for making changes and improvements. Many would argue that PDCA is *the* fundamental concept on which all improvement should be based; I can't disagree.

Shewhart (1939) had initially developed a three-stage linear process that he later modified to be cyclical. It started as specification, production, and inspection. He said it could be considered equivalent to "hypothesizing, carrying out an experiment and testing the hypothesis. The three steps constitute a dynamic scientific process of acquiring knowledge" (p. 45). Deming built on that cycle and presented it to the Japanese, who then modified it into the PDCA cycle we know today (Moen and Norman, 2010), as shown in Figure 8.1.

Deming continued to work with and on the cycle, and later modified it to PDSA, suggesting that the English word *check* was not sufficiently accurate. From my perspective, if you define the *check* appropriately, then

FIGURE 8.1
The PDCA cycle.

people will understand the purpose of that stage. Therefore, whichever acronym one chooses, and again I suggest that it is what works for you that matters, it is the thinking behind this model that underpins so much of the CI methodology in existence today.

Plan is an obvious word, or at least most would think so. The expectation in this stage is to identify and clarify the problem being solved or the potential for improvement. When problem-solving, *plan* includes the entire narrowing-down process until we get to the root cause and select the most appropriate countermeasure(s). It should include not just a plan for what to do but a clear expectation as to what the result will be and how it will be measured. This ensures the ability to check or study the result and confirm whether or not it is as expected.

Plan also delineates the *do*, not just a high-level statement as to what to do, but a detailed plan for implementation. It should include the how, not just the what. This should be an experiment, and thus, the *plan* phase is about defining the process that the experiment will follow and the expected result, the hypothesis.

Do is conducting the experiment, carrying out the planned actions to achieve the desired results. In most cases, this is where I see the emphasis: in the west, we want to see action; we want to see changes; we want to see improvements. We put a lot of effort into implementation, but often not enough to ensure that the implementation is following the plan. An often-repeated adage within the CI community is that, in the west, we simply use *plan do*, *plan do*, etc.; we seem to ignore the *check* and *act* phases of our experiments. In many cases, it's just *do*, *do*, and *do*.

Check or *study* is where we confirm the findings of our experiment. This means not just whether or not the problem was resolved, but whether it was resolved to the level we expected based on our hypothesis. In problem-solving or improvement cycles, we should be checking or studying our results against expectations. The purpose here is obviously to ensure that the problem is resolved when problem-solving but also to learn from the process. If we expected to remove all evidence of the problem but some remains, why? If we expected an improvement of 5% but only obtained 3%, then we need to ask why.

Likewise, if we expected a 5% improvement but we realized 8%, while great for our organization, if we don't study the results and our process for achieving them to understand why we obtained a greater improvement than expected, then we aren't learning, merely taking the benefit. It is only through learning that we actually improve our ability to create improvements and solve problems. It forces us to understand both the process of improvement, of experimentation, and our own processes to a much greater degree than most people are accustomed to.

The final stage of the cycle, *act*, is generally a mixture of two elements. If the experiment was successful, if we achieved the expected results, then we should standardize the new process or the change that gave us the results. Once the new process or change is standardized, we can share that knowledge with others; this is covered in Chapter 9.

If we do not achieve the expected results or they are good but not what we expected, or in some cases better than expected, then the *act* should be to review the cycle, the experiment. Some may say that you should just repeat the cycle, start over and start analyzing again to generate a new hypothesis. I think this misses the point of *check/study* and *act*. If we want to learn from our mistakes, then we need to understand where we got it wrong. Was our plan lacking in detail? Did we analyze the problem or the opportunity incorrectly? Did we miss something, or was our solution insufficient? Did we actually implement our solution according to plan? Did we take all potential factors into account?

There are many questions to ask if we do not achieve the expected result, and it is from asking these questions that we will get better at planning, implementing (doing), and of course checking or studying the result. Again, we want to improve not only our processes but also our ability to improve processes, our ability to solve problems. This comes both from experience and practice, but also from digging deep into our solutions, our processes for improvement, and understanding why things don't go as planned when this happens.

Hopefully it is obvious why Deming referred to it as the Shewhart cycle for Learning and Improvement. Both Shewhart and Deming focused on the learning aspect of it, and it is this that truly provides the long-term benefits to an organization. Too many organizations focus merely on the bottom-line benefits and ignore or downplay the importance of the learning along the way. Improving the process today is great, but if we are not learning from the process, then eventually, our ability to improve will be limited by our knowledge. The learning that takes place during problem solving and all improvement should be the focus to continuously increase our knowledge. While not insignificant, the results and the benefits to the organization are insufficient to enable ongoing improvement over time.

I once worked with a call center that was organized to maximize the time each agent spent on the phone. However, what they didn't realize was that their agents were spending a significant amount of their time on the phone speaking to answering machines. Through some basic problem solving, we found out that nobody in the organization actually understood how the dialing configuration was set up. Through the process, we were able to reduce the amount of time the agents were speaking to machines by adjusting the dialer configuration.

If we had stopped there, the improvement to the organization would have been sufficient but only for that period in time. As things change, they would need to be able to reconfigure their dialing setup frequently. The learning required to solve this initial problem enabled them to train several people in the organization, not just to adjust the dialing configuration, but also to monitor it and identify when new problems were arising. This wouldn't have happened had they only been focused on the solution to the specific problem being resolved.

It doesn't need to be like this; our inability to flex our thinking beyond specific methodologies and into deeper principles supported by whatever means fit is indicative of our historic bias toward what we know: our historic bias against the unknown and, for some reason, against new knowledge. We can challenge this bias and become learners again, if only we consciously shift focus, from improvement of things to improvement of people. What follows will be improvement in things in perpetuity, because of the improvement in people.

Tool Selection

There are a variety of other problem-solving methods or tools that exist outside the CI world. TRIZ, for example, is an innovation problem-solving methodology formulated by Russian inventor and science fiction writer Genrich Altshuller. It has been widely used across industry and has various associations throughout the world but is not associated with any specific CI methodology.

Kepner-Trague, an international training and consultancy firm, has its own problem-solving technique. Apparently they integrate this with Lean and Six Sigma methodologies, as well as work they do using their own Business Process Improvement approach.

Whatever methods or techniques you choose, the principle should be to always start with the simplest tool/technique/process in your repertoire. From a Lean perspective, that means starting with 3C and then, if the problem returns or you're unable to remove the problem using

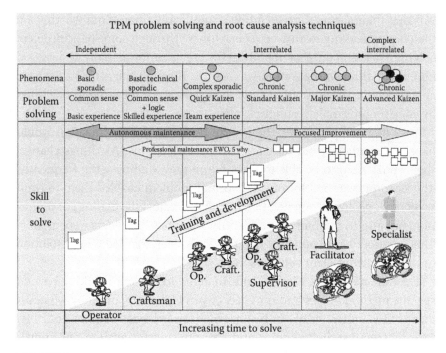

FIGURE 8.2

The hierarchy of tools. (From Johnston, C., "The Hierarchy of Tools," Kaizen Consulting and Training Services (KCTS) Ltd. Training Material, n.d.)

3C, moving on to an A3 and so on. A CI program focused on Total Productive Maintenance (TPM) uses the same approach as shown in Figure 8.2, where the more complex problems are solved using more complex methods.

Of course there is never any cut-and-dried simple rule or test to determine the best method for solving the specific problems that you face. That is why I suggest throughout this book that to gain that long-term competitive advantage, it is no longer sufficient to simply improve processes and remove waste. Companies need to learn, faster and more thoroughly than ever before, and this includes learning about how they make improvements as much as how their actual processes work.

Common versus Special Causes

Within statistics and, more specifically, Statistical Process Control, we have two types of causes of variation: common causes and special causes.

Common causes are inherent in the system; they are known and can be predicted. Special causes, on the other hand, are unknown, things we could not have predicted. For common cause problems, the root cause and solution thereof should deal with the system, be it the process, the people (training, positioning, distribution of work, etc.,—*not* individuals), or the inputs. With special-cause problems, the root cause may have nothing to do with the system; it may even be entirely out of our control. It is even possible for special-cause events to occur due to an individual, but I would suggest that this is the exception, not the rule.

Again there is significant literature available regarding statistics and these two concepts. For the purpose of this book, the primary discussion assumes that the majority of problems being faced in most organizations are common cause, systemic problems that historically have been dealt with as special-cause items. Often they are treated as fires to be put out with the assumption they are one-offs. Special causes may or may not be one-offs. Common causes definitely are not; they are a result of the processes and systems.

Root Cause Analysis

Root cause analysis is a phrase or concept that has become virtually ubiquitous throughout industry. As most people know, the conventional method for doing this is the process of asking why repeatedly until you get to the root cause, commonly called "5×Why," the premise being that we have to ask why five times to get to the root cause. However, most of my colleagues in the industry agree that it is not the number of times you ask why but the final answer that determines the root cause. Therefore, it may be five, but it may also be three, six, seven, or more whys required to get to the root cause.

The question that I get asked often, as I am sure many other consultants do, is, "How do I know when I've gotten to the root cause"? There is no simple answer to this that applies across the board. The best definition of root cause is that by removing that cause, the problem will never return. To do that, it is arguably required to change the behavior or actions that led to the current condition. This does not mean that the cause was a person's behavior. People behave as the system in which they work tells them or forces them to. People generally try to do their best in any organization in which they work. Therefore, the system will have enabled or even directed them to behave or act in a certain way, or in many cases not to do something, not to behave or act in a certain way.

An often-used example regarding a machine overload tripping out with a root cause of the oil filter being clogged with swarf provides an interesting case. If we agree that the clogged oil filter is the root cause, then replacing the oil filter, in theory, would be sufficient to remove the root cause and thus the symptom being seen, in this case, the machine tripping out. However, any mechanic knows that replacing a filter is a temporary solution to a blockage within a filter.

I would challenge that we need to understand whether or not the filter had clogged prematurely, and thus investigate what happened within the machine to cause this. If this was not the case, and the replacement of the oil filter was not done when it should have been, then this would point to a different solution. It may be that we didn't have a routine in place to change the filter; this would lead to a different solution. Thus, even in the simplest cases often provided by consultants, the most obvious answer is not always the actual answer.

Root cause analysis is an incredibly simple concept. However, as many people have found out over the years, becoming an expert is difficult. It takes practice to ensure that your root cause analysis stays on track and isn't manipulated to preconceived notions of the root cause. It takes practice to know how far to dig to ensure that the problem is solved permanently. It is unlikely that efforts to solve problems will always deliver the desired result.

People must learn how to solve problems, not just remove symptoms. This takes time, it takes practice, and it takes patience—things many organizations say they don't have. Yet the alternative, removing the symptoms only to remove them again, and again, and again as the problem resurfaces, over and over again, means that we will invest more time overall than we would have if we invested in learning. As they say, pay me now or pay me later.

One of the other comments that I have received frequently is that different people, using the same problem-solving process, will get different solutions to the same problem. This is true in many cases but not all. The reason it is true, though, is that there is no silver bullet, foolproof tool, or technique that will always point you to the root cause of every problem. The process of solving problems still needs people, and therefore, the differences in people, and their knowledge and understanding of the problem being solved, the process in which it exists, and of course the methodology being used vary. Over time, as knowledge grows throughout your organization, people's understanding of these aspects will generally converge. Sharing, discussed in the next chapter, is an indispensable way to accelerate this convergence of understanding.

Going back to my explanation of something that would change the behavior of people, we have to understand which of the causes of the filter being clogged is true. So we must ask why again. Why was the filter clogged? Somebody didn't follow the routine? Was the routine not clear? Did we have a routine for the filter to be changed at all? Did the person who should have done it know he or she should have done it? Did we have the filter in stock? Etc. If it was due to something inside the machine causing the filter to clog prematurely, then there is further investigation required. But in all other cases where it was just a failure to change the filter, then we need to understand why that wasn't done.

PROBLEM-SOLVING TOOLS

There are probably hundreds of methods for solving problems. Obviously it would be impossible to discuss all of them in any great depth in the space of this book, let alone this chapter. Traditional Lean problem-solving tools include 3C and A3 or practical problem solving (PPS). Other methods include Henrik Kjærulff's 5i; Six Sigma's Define, Measure, Analyze, Improve, and Control process or model; Ford's 8D; the World Class Manufacturing/TPM methods called Quick/Speedy Kaizen, Standard Kaizen, and Major Kaizen; Dr. Yamashima's Process Point Analysis; and so on.

Regardless of which method you choose, it should be your choice based on guidance from an expert and your own understanding of the methods and their suitability to your industry and your company. As with many of the other tools and techniques, I have seen too many organizations trying to jam a square peg into a round hole because they are using a technique that is not truly suited to their types of problems. Usually this is due to being told by a consultant that the particular method they are using is the best. But the best method for one organization may be different from the best method for another.

Some organizations have only a few high-volume manual processes; their problems will generally be related to issues within the process being repeated multiple times. Other organizations are equipment intensive, and the majority of the problems they face are related to their equipment. Some organizations have very long lead times, and their processes are vast but infrequent. The problems they face are generally individual events rather than problems that are repeated many times throughout a shift or day. Still other organizations, such as those that complete computer transactions over and over again, often find problems related to changes made to systems and procedures. Better for each organization to experiment with various methods and find the one (or few) that works best with the types of problems they have and the inherent thought processes and capabilities of the people therein.

Some of the reasons organizations should choose a single specific method or a handful of specific methods for solving problems include simplicity in training, ease of use in sharing, and enabling a focus on learning. Training is simplified because we only have to train in the one or two methods used, not the vast number of those available. It also enables individuals to become experts, true experts, in the methodology. Rather than people becoming good at many techniques, they become experts at one. A deeper knowledge and understanding results, which almost inevitably then leads to better outcomes as people become masters of their problem-solving process.

People will also be able to communicate both the solution to problems solved as well as the methodology used to get to that solution much more easily if the basic premise for how we solve problems is already understood. People no longer have to decipher the actual problem-solving methodology alongside the specific problem that was solved. The methodology has become standard, and thus, the ability to focus in on the specific problem, by those solving it and by those who are trying to learn from the solver's experience, is improved. People aren't distracted by inconsistencies between methodologies.

Yes, a changing method could be explained each time a new problem-solving method is used, but a consistent method, used throughout the organization means, that not only do we not have to explain the methodology; people will be able to follow the process much more easily. Why is this beneficial? Contrary to popular belief, any problem-solving method, just like any current standard for how we process our products or service, should be improved. Having a standard framework for solving problems also enables people to improve on the method.

Throughout this book, I have tried to make it clear that not only should an organization's processes be improved continuously; the methods used to solve problems, to share learning, to develop systems, etc., should also be improved. Yes, there are plenty of off-the-shelf tools and techniques that can be used, but if you're not looking to improve them, or at least adapt them, then there is a strong chance that you are not truly understanding them, or at least not thinking through the entirety of whatever tool is being used to fully understand its applicability to your organization and the environment in which you operate.

3C/4C

3C/4C is not so much a problem-solving tool or technique, but a series of words, all beginning with C, that guide the problem solver through a thinking process. The three Cs are *concern*, *cause*, and *countermeasure*, although some have added *containment* as a fourth C, between *cause* and *countermeasure*, to remind people that sometimes, it is necessary to contain a problem temporarily until a full and proper solution can be identified and implemented.

Arguably one of the simplest methods for solving problems, many suggest that this should be the first method used for all problems. This is based on the idea that many problems do not require extensive investigation or analysis, because the cause and countermeasure can be simply deduced by looking at the problem.

A3/Practical Problem Solving

The A3/PPS template shown in Figure 8.3 is probably the single most widely known and used tool or technique for solving problems, especially within the Lean consultancy community and those organizations that are practicing Lean. It is primarily a format for reporting the results of the problem-solving process. However, the process provides a great guide for the thinking required and enables users to follow the flow step by step. This makes problems easier to solve than by merely considering the elements and attempting to solve the problem without following the thought process and only using it for final reporting.

Figure 8.3 is one of many A3 templates I have seen over the years, suggesting that many have decided that the format they were provided or first

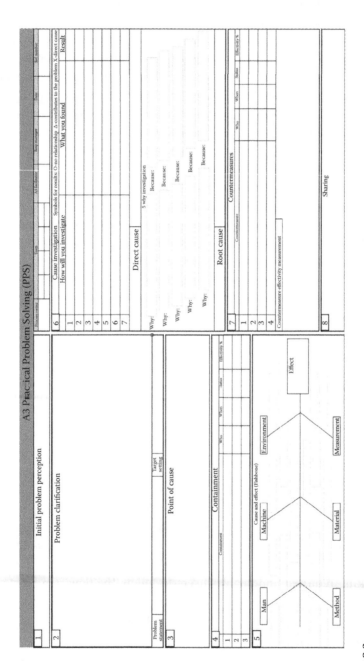

FIGURE 8.3
One of many A3/PPS templates.

came across was not exactly suited for their organization. Many may criticize this modification of the original tool; however, if we're not challenging our improvement process, then I argue that we do not fully understand it. This doesn't mean we have to modify everything, but that we must test its suitability and fully explore possibilities rather than accept everything at face value.

I can't remember exactly where I read or heard it, but I believe the reason that the A3 size was selected had nothing to do with it being optimal for representing the problem-solving process. It was because at the time, much of the communication within Toyota across factories and other locations was through *fax* machines—and at the time (and probably still today), the A3 was the largest size of paper that could be faxed. I know that when I worked in Toyota, we often reported our problem-solving process and results on a piece of card much larger than A3. The point is, like in many other cases, the original thinking that went into the design of the various tools does not mean that they are sacrosanct and cannot be challenged or modified to suit.

Of course, most Lean purists will say the A3 or PPS template is the preferred method for solving problems. It is a fantastic technique, but I believe it is more appropriate for certain types of problems than others. It is best suited for problems with multiple occurrences such as damages or defects, which is why most examples provided during training exercises are of defects found. Single-event problems can be solved using A3, but often, the lack of data for single events makes narrowing down the problem through stratification difficult or impossible. The narrowing down often establishes a time line of the event(s), and the investigation is often a series of interviews with those involved. There is little if any stratification involved when the problem is a one-time event.

There are many problems where A3 and the thinking that is required to follow the process do not provide the user with sufficient instruction or guidance to gather necessary information. There is an assumption that people will know not just where to look but also how. In manual processes with manual problems, it can be as simple as going to watch somebody perform the process. When machines are involved, it can be difficult, if not impossible, to truly understand what is causing the problem without high-speed video, detailed understanding of the mechanisms and how they work together, or specific information regarding limitations and tolerances of components, tooling, materials, etc. A3 does not provide detail into how to collect that information, only on how to represent it and, in many cases, how to analyze it.

Many of the TPM-based problem-solving tools provide much more guidance for digging deep into problems to understand what is causing machine faults, whether they are quality or performance problems. These techniques were designed specifically for these types of problems. Additionally, TPM-based problem solving also includes guidance on analyzing material failure modes. A3 will not help a user identify the difference between broken bolts due to torsion compared to tension or compression, for example.

Regardless of some of the limitations, A3 remains one of the best methods for solving most problems that people will encounter in their daily routines.

The 5i Technique

I've included Henrik Kjærulff's 5i problem-solving method (shown in Figure 8.4) in this chapter, not because I think it is a superior method for solving problems but because Henrik had the courage to put it out there as a simpler alternative to A3 for people new to problem solving.

This type of evolution in the application of principles is essential for the CI community to continue to build our knowledge and understanding, not just of what we do, but of why and how we do it. To improve our ability to work with people to improve their processes, we must also be open and willing, even looking for new ways to improve our own approach, our own tools and techniques. I would challenge any leader embarking on a journey toward CI: if your consultant is still doing things the same way he or she did 15 years ago, then the question needs to be asked, "How much can this person help me to improve if they are not improving themselves?"

SUMMARY

While this has been a very brief overview of the principles, tools, and techniques available for solving problems, the intent was to demonstrate that while they are good tools, they are not the only ones. What is important to an organization is not which tool they use, but that the tool they use fits their organization, and that they understand not just how to use it, but why it works for them. It is the principle of solving problems to root cause and learning about the problem and the process it sits within, as well as

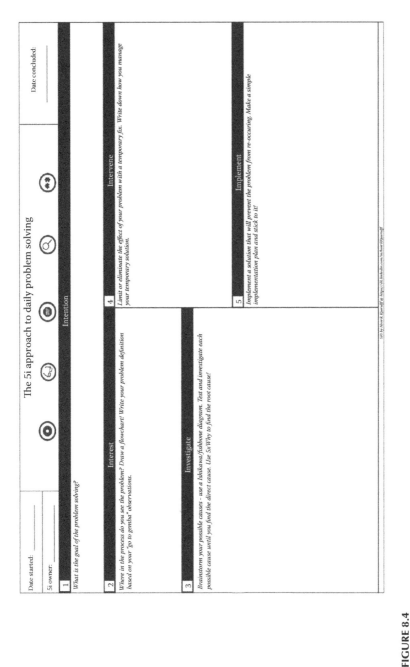

FIGURE 8.4

The 5i problem-solving template. (From Kjærulff, H., "The 5i Approach to Daily Problem Solving," https://www.linkedin.com/pulse/5i-approach-daily-problem-solving-henrik-kj%C3%A6rulff?trk=mp-reader-card, 2016.)

the methods used to solve the problem, that is key. Problem solving, like many things, is simple in concept but often very difficult in real life.

Some people are better than others at solving problems. The challenge should be, how can we ensure that their knowledge and skill is used to develop others within the organization to build capability across the board? That is the question that we should be asking. It is the capability that is important, not the results from the problem solving itself. Don't get me wrong; that too is important, but if we're not building that capability across the organization, then we are limiting our improvement to the handful of people who are capable.

The reality is that most people are capable if we just give them the chance to learn how. Through practice and coaching, people will begin thinking for themselves again yet follow the clear guidance provided through coaching regarding the objectives you want to achieve.

The tools can help as they provide a means for sharing knowledge, for sharing understanding of what we are trying to achieve, but they are insufficient. We need to build capability, and this comes from a deeper understanding than just how to do something; we need to understand why we do it the way we do it. We need to focus our efforts on learning as much as on removing the root cause and resolving the problem.

It is through learning that our knowledge grows and thus our capability grows. Einstein has been cited as saying, "The thinking that created the problem cannot be used to solve the problem." Although I've been unable to find a reliable source to confirm that this actually came from Einstein, the premise is appropriate. We need to get people thinking, thinking differently. This comes from challenging our problems, facing them head on, but it also comes from challenging our processes, including our problem-solving processes.

In the next chapter, I'll discuss various ways for sharing the knowledge gained through our problem solving. It is this sharing that accelerates the learning across the organization, increasing our speed of knowledge building.

9

Sharing New Knowledge

The third principle of dynamic organizations is the concept of sharing knowledge gained from solving the problems that arise. I previously mentioned the "learn once, apply many times" principle. This principle is simple; why should everyone have to learn everything on his or her own? Why not let one individual or team learn the lesson and teach (*share* with) the rest of the organization? This sharing happens regardless of what you do; better then to coach and guide it to ensure that it is focused on improving the organization as opposed to learning how to hide problems, how to play the system.

Of course the concept is simple, as many great concepts are, but the application, for whatever reason, seems to have been lost on so many. How do we go about sharing what we learn with the rest of our organization? Firstly, it is actually rare to need to share what you learned with the entire organization. Most organizations have many functions that perform a variety of tasks. The sharing necessary is usually confined to others who perform the same or similar tasks.

Therefore, the first consideration with regard to *share* is whether or not to share, and with whom should we share. Of course, I can't answer that here, but I can give some guidance. The first principle with this is to share anything that can be useful to others. Of course, that could just about cover everything or everyone, at least if you learned something valuable while solving a problem. However, we need to think beyond "everyone and everything," or we'll not have much time for more problem solving because we will be too busy sharing.

Obviously anyone involved with the process where the problem occurred and was solved should be informed of the root cause and the solution, even if the solution is invisible to them, such as when the root cause of the problem was actually in an area outside of where the symptom was being seen.

This gives some reassurance (or not in some cases) that the symptom will not be seen again. People want to know not just that a problem is solved, but how it was solved; in some cases, this desire to know stems from a distrust of others' problem-solving abilities. They want to get that warm fuzzy feeling that the solution is actually fit for purpose and will ensure that the problem won't arise again.

Even if it is just the solution that is shared out, it is good to have everyone looking out for the symptom to ensure that the solution actually works. I've seen countless solutions to problems fail, not because they weren't investigated properly, or that the solution was implemented incorrectly, but because people are people, and not everyone adapts to changes or solutions as quickly or as robustly as everyone else. We have to expect that people will tend to revert to old habits for a variety of reasons.

Part of management's role, as will be discussed in Chapter 10, is to coach and develop their people; this includes ensuring that changes are incorporated into everyone's routines. Process confirmation is an invaluable tool for creating coaching conversations where managers can reinforce changes in routines, changes in standards. But managers can't be everywhere all the time. They also rely on their front line to be their eyes and ears on a continual basis. This does not exempt them from being out there; it merely supports them when they can't be out there.

Apart from those who work in the area where the symptom was seen, those who work where the root cause was found should also be informed of the necessary changes to ensure that the solution is fully implemented. For obvious reasons, if one area of a business is causing problems to another area of the business when the root cause is found and a solution identified and implemented, those who work in that area that was causing the issue must be informed of the solution. If the problem solving was done properly, at least one of the members of this area would have been involved, and thus, sharing the new knowledge is not difficult. There are a variety of methods, as you will see further on in this chapter.

Now that we've shared with the area that saw the problem and the area that caused the problem (yes, in many cases, they are one and the same), there are potentially several other areas of the business where the new knowledge would be useful. Any area where people do similar tasks or where the technology is comparable (if part of the issue was within the technology) is next in line for sharing. Many problems are universal. The knowledge gained from solutions to problems that resulted in accidents or safety incidents is almost always useful to every employee within the business.

There is no silver bullet rule or guide that can be given to ensure that all information necessary is shared with all the appropriate people in the business. It is for leaders and their teams to decide with whom to share. However, I would suggest that the default position is as wide as practical. In one engagement I worked on, there were three sites that did the exact same activity. Whenever we solved a problem that the site I was working in had, I tried to get the local management team to share with the other two sites. There was strong resistance to this, and I'm not absolutely certain why, but my guess was that they were embarrassed or afraid of being embarrassed by admitting that they had actually had the problem in the first place.

Of course there is nothing I can write in this book or even teach you face to face that will reduce this concern, but I urge you to consider the impact on your business from the fear of embarrassment. The willingness to stand in front of your peers and admit you had a problem is a great trait. It must, however, be supported by management. They should be, as we will discuss in Chapter 10, supporting and developing their people to make problems obvious, solve problems, and share what is learned in the process. Part of this supporting and coaching is likely to include demonstrating, including demonstrating that having problems is normal and acceptable (or even desirable). Remember, problems are a good thing; they enable us to learn, improve, and grow as individuals. "Having no problems is the biggest problem of all" (Ohno, 2006).

If people are too embarrassed to do this, then the vast amount of learning that should take place will not. Instead, the historic hiding of problems and downplaying the truth to save face will continue. Organizations will continue to believe the various lies and half-truths being told to protect egos and, more dangerous for your organization, to protect careers. Growth in knowledge and thus capability will slow, if not stop. The politics that create the atmosphere where people are afraid of either embarrassment or a negative impact on their career from admitting to problems is carcinogenic to organizations.

TRADITIONAL LEAN TOOLS

There are a variety of Lean tools already mentioned (making problems obvious) in SEE that also provide the ability to share new knowledge.

Whenever the problem solved is in a frontline process with a detailed standard in place, or when a new standard is created for a process, the standard itself is a great mechanism for sharing knowledge. Of course standards are not, in and of themselves, sufficient if they are not readily available and regularly used by those that undertake the work.

In many cases, the knowledge gained is that the original or most recent version of the standard, as written, was insufficient or lacked clarity or otherwise didn't cover every likely scenario, not that it will ever be possible to do so. However, as you gain more and more knowledge about your processes and systems, you can gradually increase the available information for others.

Of course there has to be a balance and some level of sanity in this area. Nobody will ever read or even look at your standards if they make *War and Peace* look like a mere anecdote. Having said that, when I was a helicopter mechanic, the standards for performing maintenance covered several walls in our technical publications library, not sheets of paper on the walls, but manuals as thick as bricks. We learned very quickly how to use them and which sections were most relevant to the work we performed regularly. In fact, learning to use the manuals was one of the key lessons bestowed upon the new members of our team as they began to develop their skills in maintaining aircraft.

When people joined the unit from their training, they were in essence treated as apprentices. They will have learned the basics of maintenance and had an overview of the specifics of our aircraft, but in most cases, they hadn't actually done much work on any aircraft. They would be assigned to work with a seasoned mechanic whose standard response to questions about assembly sequences, tools required, torque values, etc., was "look it up." This was not because seasoned mechanics didn't know; they may or may not have. But the expectation was that everyone would be very familiar with the manuals.

Certain items were expected to be looked up every time: things change as a result of previous problem-solving evolutions, and it was important to ensure that whatever changes had been incorporated into the manuals were practiced in the work. So new people quickly learned both the value of the manuals (our standard) and how to use them.

Of course, not every job requires this level of detailed specifications. Many processes are reasonably simple and the standards required do not fill an entire wall. For many frontline operators, the required standards to complete their daily tasks could fit on a handful of standard-sized sheets of paper. We discussed these in detail in Chapter 7, so I won't go into further detail on standards in that respect, but standards are a great tool for sharing the knowledge gained from solving a problem.

Other than standards, changes to various andons, kanbans, Kamishibai cards, etc., can also be used to share new knowledge, but I would argue that merely changing the process, the light, the sound, etc., is insufficient for communicating and actually sharing the knowledge. People need to know not just that things have changed, but how and why they changed. Remember, "People don't buy what you do; they buy why you do it." This is true with changes to process as much as changes to the overall business strategy.

This leads nicely to the shift start-up meeting, the information center review, or whatever other regular performance review meetings take place, especially at the team level. I'll discuss general meetings later, but within the "Traditional Lean Tools" section, we should include the visual management center (VMC) review as a mechanism for sharing new knowledge gained.

From my perspective, this method is only inferior to *yokoten* and individual coaching. Yokoten is discussed further on in this chapter; it is arguably a Lean tool, but I've left it out of the "Traditional Lean Tools" section because I have yet to see any other organization or consultant discuss or otherwise engage this tool in the 15 years I have been working in this industry.

In simplest terms, the shift start-up meetings or whatever other titles we have for them are, in essence, the same as the smaller meetings discussed later on, where 5–10 people can discuss the change, the solution, the new standard, and thus the new knowledge in sufficient depth to answer questions, to provide demonstrations if appropriate, to go to the actual place to see the solution or change, etc.

It is a very good method for sharing knowledge, yet many organizations have these meeting structures with limited actual benefit. It is not the fact that a meeting takes place or that information is transmitted that matters. It is the learning that must take place, the actual transfer of knowledge, not just the passing of information. It is not good enough to read out a paragraph or two describing the new solution. We must fully understand the story and ensure that the entire team understands the message. The problem, the solution, the change required, the method for getting there, etc. That is sharing knowledge.

READ-AND-INITIAL BOARDS

Updating standards, whether standardized work sheets or standard operating procedures or whatever your organization calls its standards, requires informing people of the update, or at least that the standards have been updated. One of the easiest ways to manage changes or updates is the read-and-initial board: a simple visual system that existed long before e-mail and computers that makes it easy to provide information to all. While I was in the Marines, these were used primarily for pilots to ensure they knew about various restrictions on airspace, live firing ranges, meteorological conditions, etc.

Read-and-initial boards are simple to set up. Figure 9.1 is an example of a read-and-initial board. Down the left-hand column you list the names of the people in the area or those whom the potential changes will affect. Across the top row, you add the changes or lessons as they become effective or are necessary to share. You can have additional information such as date entered, expected sign-off dates, etc., if you feel it's necessary.

Read and initial

	04-Oct	06-Oct	06-Oct	28-Oct	15-Nov		
	Holiday Closure	*STD 4.2 Update*	*STD 6.12 Update*	*Tool Control Update*	*STD 2.6 Update*		
J. Blogs	*JB*	*JB*	*JB*				
T. Ford	*TF*	*TF*	*TF*	*TF*	*TF*		
A. Nother	*AN*	*AN*	*AN*	*AN*	*AN*		
T. Blogs	*TB*	*TB*	*TB*				
B. Newman	*BN*	*BN*	*BN*	*BN*	*BN*		
C. Johnson	*CJ*	*CJ*	*CJ*	*CJ*	*CJ*		

FIGURE 9.1
An example read-and-initial board.

Once the system is up and running, as items are added, the expectation is that the individuals listed in the left-hand column will check the board periodically and initial that they have read and understood the content of whatever information is posted. This not only shares the knowledge; it also provides a simple visual mechanism for making problems obvious. In this case, the problem would be people unaware of an item.

These read-and-initial boards are probably the least proactive form of *share* I would support. You provide a copy of the information, usually the standard or sometimes a memo or other note, and the tracking sheet with everyone's name listed; they initial against the item when they are aware of and understand it.

E-MAIL

In the age of e-mail, it seems to be the preferred method for communicating everything and anything. E-mail can be great in some respects. It provides an individual document that the receivers can read when it is convenient for them. They can then store or discard the information as they see fit, and if they store it in any sort of reasonable filing system, they can refer back to it as and when it is necessary. However, like all of the other written forms of *share*, it lacks the personal touch, the ability for the receiver to see the specific details, and of course provides the potential for either misunderstanding, no understanding, and in many cases, not being read at all.

E-mails provide little if any accountability—they provide the option to be read or not. Certainly, we can ask for a read receipt, but many people set those up on automatic. Otherwise, it becomes another task, albeit small, added to the already overloaded inbox. A read-and-initial board can easily be verified, and delinquency can be challenged. Sure, people could initial without reading, but they should be held accountable for having or knowing the information. It is a proactive confirmation that cannot be automated in Outlook or whatever e-mail platform you use.

MEETINGS

Obviously we can also discuss, or at least present, the changes in team meetings or other gatherings. Depending on the size of your team, this may or may not be a good approach for sharing knowledge. Side conversations, time to digest, and messages before or afterward all may detract from the absorption of the information. In smaller teams, this is not usually an issue, but trying to brief 150 people about changes to a standard is likely to be ineffectual. Better to do it in small groups of 5–10, where people can ask questions and the person sharing the information can confirm understanding or at least the appearance of understanding.

In many cases, it is possible, and almost always desirable, to share the new knowledge at the location where it actually applies. Rather than getting everyone into an office or meeting room, take them to the location where the change has been made. Whether it is a new layout for material storage (yes, Lean organizations still store material), a new method of assembling a part, the new procedures for filling in various forms, the new script for answering inbound calls, or whatever, make it real by demonstrating the actual change, as often as possible.

LITTLE BLACK BOOKS

Other than updating or improving standards, or in some cases creating them in the first place, there are several good options for sharing knowledge gained throughout an organization. Little black books can be good if they are used by a handful of people, not one each but a shared booklet with tips, tricks, and rules of thumb learned along the way. Little black books for individuals are anathema to dynamic organizations. They allow individuals to hoard knowledge.

The little gems of knowledge gained over the years can be incredibly beneficial if the little black books are filled with the specific principles and practices that are inherent in your industry, organization, processes, etc. Even things such as lists of the acronyms used in your organization can be useful to others, and thus, capturing them in a single place enables faster sharing of the information, as well as the ability, if it is properly organized, for people to search for specific items or bits of information that would be expected to lie within these little black books.

Toyota uses these types of books in their design engineering functions for things such as radius limitations on curved panels, thickness requirements near edges, etc. (Morgan and Liker, 2006).

SHARED SERVICES FILES/PROGRAMS

My least favorite method for sharing knowledge is SharePoint! What a fantastic concept and tool, but not a great way to share learning. I've seen many organizations create a SharePoint (or similar) site so people could search to see what others had done or learned in dealing with the problems they faced, in the hopes that they might find something that they could use rather than having to figure it out themselves.

Of course, that is what we are trying to do with *share*, make it so that others can learn from our learning, not force them to learn for themselves, but SharePoint is *not* a good mechanism for doing that. Yes, it ticks the box on audits, but that's only because auditors either don't understand what we are trying to accomplish or don't care sufficiently to challenge an ineffective system.

To begin with, the organizing system needs to be universally understood, but this is virtually impossible given the nature of the work carried out in diverse teams across organizations. I've already mentioned Mooers' law in Chapter 7. The more difficult it is for people to find something useful, the less likely they are to try.

SharePoint becomes a cumbersome virtual file cabinet where everything goes and nobody looks, and yet we still believe we are sharing our knowledge. I know that SharePoint has its uses, but how valuable is it to file 27,000+ improvements or "lessons learned" documents in the hopes that when someone is looking for other examples similar to their own, they will find something within those 27,000+ documents? Would you spend hours opening and closing any file that has a title or keyword that sounds like something related to your problem? I wouldn't; I've tried, but I've quickly realized that this mechanism is great for keeping records but doesn't actually enable easy learning by others.

Yes, it is possible, and there will undoubtedly be several anecdotal stories where someone did actually find something useful and apply it to his or her area of a business. However, it has been my experience, supported by hundreds of frontline employees' feedback, that finding anything useful within these systems is virtually impossible. Luck is about the only technique that consistently enables success in sharing through these shared filing programs.

Secondly, a one-pager, or worse, a several-page document explaining the problem, the process to get to the root cause, the solution, and the results, although great for supporting learning, should not be the sole mechanism for that learning. A3 reports, A3 problem-solving sheets (practical problem solving [PPS]), and various other single-page or single-point lessons (SLPs) or one-page or one-point lessons (OPLs) are best used as visuals supporting a lesson, not the lesson in and of itself.

They can be misunderstood depending on the information provided within, and people will generally only include the positive results achieved. You will learn much more from hearing about, seeing, and asking about the process and the failures along the way than you will by reading about the final result. Of course, this applies to e-mails, read-and-initial boards, and any other written form of sharing. The ideal is always verbal, face to face, with a visit to the affected location where possible.

INTRANET SITES

Similar to SharePoint, intranet sites can be useful in many ways. Depending on how they are used, they can be effective ways for sharing certain lessons from changes made and problems solved. If there is a running dialogue from each department that discusses changes and problems and solutions, then it can be effective. I would argue that in most cases, these are good for large-scale problems that impact the entire business.

On one project I worked on, though, the interim results of the project were published on the company intranet site, and shortly afterward, I heard grumblings and rumors from frontline workers who believed, and rightly so, that the information provided on the site was biased and inaccurate. The article had created a positive picture of a major change in their area of the business, and it suggested high levels of engagement from the front line, significant benefits to the company, etc. While this wasn't entirely false, it wasn't entirely true either. It was, as many internal articles are, an exaggeration of the truth in order to promote the site, the change, and the internal organization that had supported and championed the change.

Intranet sites can be effective, but like SharePoint, they are broad-brush approaches that work for certain types of communication but not all. If you use this approach to share new knowledge, be sure that the message is fit for the entire audience, not just the executive who wants to hear a good news story. That is definitely *not* what we are trying to achieve in *share*.

NEWSLETTERS

Similar to company intranet sites, some units in various businesses I have worked in have a regular newsletter. I have even been a part of introducing them in some of my clients' sites. They can be very effective in informing about site-wide or functional changes, but they are not really suited for detailed process changes or updates to standards at the front line.

Where I have seen these as effective mechanisms for sharing knowledge, they were widely read by all employees. This requires them to be not just informative but also interesting. Having personal stories and outside interests can help with getting people to read them. If they are merely the humdrum management speak covering the state of the business, people will read them but not necessarily with the same interest or open mind that you will want if using this as a forum for communicating changes or lessons learned.

YOKOTEN

My favorite, and arguably the best, mechanism for sharing knowledge is what the Japanese call yokoten—roughly translated, it means "across everywhere." It's about spreading knowledge widely but also effectively. I set up such a practice when I worked with an aerospace client. They had a decent improvement program, but their mechanism for sharing results was SharePoint. On several occasions, people came to me with their frustrations from being told to look for examples within their SharePoint, only to come back empty handed; they said it was virtually impossible to find something useful.

I started with the team leaders, getting them together each week and having a couple of them prepared in advance to present solutions to problems or improvements made in their areas. We'd visit the areas of the presenting team leaders so they could show the others the specifics. Several times, improvements would spread to other areas from team leader to team leader because they didn't just read a document; they were shown the old, the change, and the results. They were able to ask questions and fully understand both the change and the impact of the change on the other area in the business. They were able to discuss the process and understand the mistakes made along the way.

After the process was up and running, I then invited the managers to come along and see what was going on in their areas. Some were keen verbally but rarely showed up; others were there consistently. Those that didn't attend regularly missed not only an opportunity to support their team leaders but also an opportunity to challenge, to coach, and most importantly, to learn. Obviously, those that did turn up regularly were very engaged with their areas and were keen to capitalize on opportunities to coach and develop their people to further improve their areas of the business. They were also eager to identify opportunities from other areas. There may be nothing better than having someone present a problem he or she faced and the solution he or she found when you yourself are facing a similar problem: what a gem!

Following the success of that system in the engine shop where I was working, I suggested to the continuous improvement (CI) leads in the other business units that we do the same for our monthly CI review. Why do we sit in an office and discuss what has happened and where we are in each area? Why don't we go into a different business unit each time and show each other the changes we've made, the solutions we've found to various problems faced? What was most interesting was that these guys were the other CI leads in their business units, and when I first suggested we actually leave the office and go and see for ourselves, the responses were not what I expected. A couple of them were up for it, of course, but those that still held some traditional management views were nervous. Maybe they were nervous because the things they had been reporting were not as good as they had been reporting them to be.

Either way, it was agreed, and we began visiting the different business units each month. Various business unit representatives latched on to certain items so they could take them back to their units, and some items were just interesting. I'm certain that some were not interesting at all, but nobody said this was perfect! The point of this, though, is that people actually go and see the change, and are then in a much better position to learn about both the change and the process that was followed in identifying, implementing, and cementing the change, whatever it was.

SUMMARY

Throughout this chapter, we have discussed a variety of methods for communicating and sharing knowledge across organizations. While there is no perfect method that engages with everyone and ensures absolute saturation of all new knowledge, some are better than others. If you truly want to accelerate the speed of learning in your organization, then it is the way you share new knowledge that is most important.

With the right structure in place, with appropriate spans of control in your frontline teams, you can share new knowledge quickly and broadly. If we practice what we preach in terms of human beings being our most important asset, then we should be investing in them and the continual increase in knowledge required to keep up or, better yet, to set the pace in our industry. This investment costs much less than one might think. An hour a week is generally more than sufficient for sharing new knowledge.

This hour can be spent reading and writing documents and uploading photos, or it can be spent engaging with people, showing them the whole story, and ensuring understanding and the creation and evolution of new knowledge.

In the next chapter, I will discuss how leaders' roles have changed, that they can't continue to ignore development or abdicate responsibility of it to training departments. Leaders need to become coaches; they need to stop solving the problems themselves and start teaching and coaching their people to do these things for themselves.

10

Show—The Importance of Coaching and Developing Your People

INTRODUCTION

Much of the discussion and literature regarding failed implementations of Lean revolves around the failure of leadership to fully engage with the program. There is much truth behind this, and as argued earlier, it is one of the main factors that cause Lean programs to underdeliver. This under-delivery comes from lower levels of initial improvements as well as a lack of sustainability of whatever improvements are achieved.

Even when the senior leadership is not engaged and will not engage, that does not mean that the implementation cannot deliver significant results and become sustainable. However, this requires a different approach, as discussed earlier. Executives must move away from focusing on immediate results, away from the requirement to deliver return on investment (ROI) rapidly. This doesn't mean that your organization won't get results, or that the ROI will not be positive; it will, if you focus on building capability over immediate returns.

When it comes to leadership, there is a specific capability that matters for them beyond the first three capabilities. They need to be able to coach and develop their people to do those three things. They need to be open to, even focused on, allowing people to fail, to make mistakes, to experiment and learn along the way. The most important question they can ask along the way is, "What did you learn"?

Of course, there are other questions to ask and other ways to elicit a similar reflection from your staff, but the general role of leadership within an organization practicing Lean is to coach and to develop their people. Invest in them, and the returns will be phenomenal. Ignore them at your peril. To begin with, the organization will need to understand that coaching and developing people also inherently requires a certain amount of autonomy for those being coached and developed. They have to be able to experiment, to make mistakes, and to learn from them. The leader as coach is not there to ensure that everything always goes well, but to ensure that learning takes place regardless of whether things go well or poorly.

AUTONOMY, MASTERY, AND PURPOSE

Since we are mentioning autonomy, it's worth reminding you that according to the scientific evidence, as discussed in Dan Pink's (2009b) book *Drive*, autonomy is one of the trifecta of motivators for people. The other two are mastery and purpose. In terms of purpose, Pink says people need to feel like they are doing something important, something bigger than themselves. Leaders can create this purpose with their mission and vision for the organization. Not the vision statement, or the mission statement, but the actual vision, the actual mission, one that actually means something to people. Think of JFK's mission to send someone to the moon and return him or her home safely. Quite powerful, that purpose flowed all the way to the janitor, who is often quoted as saying he is helping to put a man on the moon.

Purpose can be provided for employees and incorporated into everything they do. They need to do little work to get it; they just have to be open to whatever is set out by the leadership. There are plenty of books on that subject, so I won't go into it here. However, in principle, there is not a great deal that needs to be done on a daily basis to create purpose. The most effective mechanism is not posters, plaques, or other posted information though. Ideally whatever message or purpose you want to engender in your organization is simple enough to incorporate into your daily language.

On a recent training course I was facilitating, some delegates from a national grocery chain suggested a simple statement for their purpose—"feeding the nation." How easy would it be to incorporate that phrase into our daily conversations? How easy would it be to bring that concept, that idea, that purpose into everything they do? In simplest terms, purpose is about creating an emotional connection to the work being done.

For mastery, people need to feel like they are getting better and better at something, although not necessarily the same something. This sits very nicely within a Lean organization, where the focus is on learning. True, people can get better and better at creating standardized work, at changing over from one product to another, at making kanban cards, but true mastery comes from greater knowledge, not just greater experience. It requires actual learning along the way.

Mastery is slightly more difficult to provide if the people in your organization do the same things day in and day out. They can usually become masters quite quickly, and then what? This is where Lean really comes into its own. But it requires the third element of motivation as posited by Pink, autonomy.

By giving people the autonomy to develop their roles and the way they do them, they can become masters of improvement, masters of developing better systems and processes that highlight problems earlier and earlier, easier and easier. They can become master problem solvers, and they can become experts at sharing knowledge.

Realizing that even the most straightforward simple task can be improved is not difficult. Most managers can see opportunities to improve many of the processes their people do. What is lacking, though, is the release of authority from manager to employee, the delegation of ownership of the process.

Yes, there are legal and/or technical limitations as to how far this can go. Yet, too many managers continue to lack trust in their people to do what is right for the organization where they can. They are unwilling or feel unable to truly give their people the autonomy to make changes to how things are done. Quite possibly, this comes from the fear of reprisal if and when things go wrong. Keeping experiments small limits the risk to the organization.

Frederick Taylor suggested that it was the manager's job to identify and implement the best method for each task. This completely removed any element of autonomy and engagement from the front line. As previously discussed, this is part of the history of industry, which seems to remain in many organizations, the distrust and lower opinions of the front line, which means they are not given the opportunity and freedom to influence their daily life.

Not only does this lack of empowerment, autonomy, freedom, etc., drive lack of engagement; it also limits what the organization can achieve. Put simply, you can either have a handful of people coming up with ideas and making improvements or have everyone doing so. Yes, there will be mistakes, and there will be setbacks, but the leader's role is to coach and develop his or her people along the way to ensure that they are learning with each failure, with each setback. You might also find yourself quite surprised by how knowledgeable and ingenious the frontline folks actually are.

The iceberg of ignorance presented in Chapter 2, while debatable in terms of absolute accuracy, is a sound principle. Yes, as McManis (2016) suggests, there are also problems that the front lines are not aware of, but the principle of hidden problems is not wrong. Too many organizations have too many problems hidden away behind politics, behind egos, and behind the scenes, where the work actually gets done.

Not only do most frontline workers have a solid grasp of the organization's biggest processing problems, they also have novel solutions in mind. They may not be aware of entity-wide issues or issues facing the organization from an external perspective, but they'll know what is wrong internally. And although some of their ideas may be cost prohibitive, or unworkable given the overall direction the organization is heading, it is the leader's job to guide their thinking and their solutions to ensure they fit within the overall principles of making problems obvious.

By giving the front line the autonomy they desire alongside the ownership and accountability required to enable them to experiment and learn, the organization will reap the rewards of an army of problems solvers. Having everyone focused on making things better rather than just on making things means you're multiplying your potential by the number of people in your organization, not just the number of people in your management team. The rewards will be greater by far than will be the case if you continue the command-and-control approach and limit the input from the front line to a handful of ideas that go through committee-like approval processes and then become the problem of management to implement.

The ownership of any new solution, regardless of how good it is, will continue to stay with the management if the autonomy to own the improvement from idea through to implementation is not real. Many organizations know this and have known it for decades. They have coached and developed their people long before they had heard of or understood the concepts of Lean. They have empowered their people and enabled them to affect change, to improve the various aspects of the work. What follow are a couple of examples of organizations I have worked in and how they ensure that their leaders are developing their people.

UNITED STATES MARINE CORPS

Contrary to popular belief, the United States Marine Corps (USMC) does not create robot troops who don't think for themselves. Quite the opposite happens, and that begins in boot camp. Yes, there is an expectation that orders are followed and that Marines follow certain principles and guidance from headquarters. However, combat training as well as other elements of training in whatever specialty field Marines enter, and courses and programs they attend throughout their careers, however long they are, generally teach principles and concepts rather than strict rules that must be followed.

There are standards in every aspect of Marine Corps life, very specific standards about uniforms, courtesies, and procedures for obtaining gear, even for how to go on holiday, vacation, or "leave" as it was called. But that doesn't mean that Marines don't do an awful lot of thinking for themselves. One of the core concepts that Marines are taught, and you might have seen it portrayed in a variety of films, is to improvise, adapt, and overcome.

Marines are taught to think for themselves following the concept of Mission Command as developed by Helmuth Von Moltke and discussed in Chapter 2. The Marines understand that although the objective can be set from headquarters, the tactics required at the front line will vary from location to location, day to day, even minute to minute, and it is the ability to think for themselves that makes frontline troops so effective. They are taught the basic principles and a variety of techniques and tactics to achieve the objective, but the specific tactics chosen on the ground depend on the situation at hand. This should be true in business just as it is in combat, albeit in a different manner and to a different extent.

Although the style of coaching within the Marines might put off a few folks, it is very effective for the types of people who sign up for the Marines. There is, of course, the need to create a certain element of "robot" order following. In situations where people are less inclined to follow instructions that are potentially fatal, the discipline that when orders are given, they are followed is essential. However, the "how" for most orders is open for Marines to determine themselves. We were encouraged to use our initiative to make things happen. It was rare to be told exactly how to do something. Normally, the objective was given, but the latitude for how to accomplish it was left to the individuals.

If we made a mistake, which happened often, the common retort was "good initiative, bad judgment." When this happened, it was often the case that the leader would spend a bit of time with the Marine exploring the thinking process that led to the decision to undertake that specific action, not to berate or otherwise ridicule the Marine, but to help him or her understand his or her thinking and to find common ground to build on for future decisions.

Throughout their careers, Marines are often intentionally put into situations that require them to think through a variety of options and to come up with a plan to achieve the mission. In many cases, it was only the mission or objective that was stated, without any specific instructions as to how to achieve it. Many training exercises are run almost entirely with clear objectives, a bit of guidance on where to start, and the rest is left to the small units. The standard debrief at the end is all about, What did we learn? What did we do well? and What could we do better next time?

Yes, there was a high level of competition between units, but the objective throughout peacetime training, alongside competence in basic and advanced skills, is to develop the underlying thinking that will be used when the eventual conflict begins. It is all about getting Marines to think for themselves, not to blindly follow orders.

Of course there is a framework around much of this coaching and development. The USMC uses principle-based leadership to get Marines to focus on the values that the Marine Corps believes are most important to its mission. It is not merely about traits, and while there is a huge expectation that results will be delivered, that missions will be accomplished, there is also an expectation that when this isn't the case, that there is a significant amount of learning in the process.

There are 11 leadership principles that all Marines learn in boot camp. They are regularly used in personal challenges by seniors, peers, and occasionally junior troops challenging their seniors when the senior is not living up to the principles.

USMC Leadership Principles

Be technically and tactically proficient.
Know yourself and seek self-improvement.
Know your Marines and look out for their welfare.
Keep your Marines informed.
Set the example.
Ensure that assigned tasks are understood, supervised, and accomplished.
Train your Marines as a team.
Make sound and timely decisions.
Develop a sense of responsibility among subordinates.
Employ your command in accordance with its capabilities.
Seek responsibility and take responsibility for your actions.

Interestingly, the second principle, "Know yourself and seek self-improvement," is probably more closely aligned with the Japanese meaning of the term *kaizen* than most westerners are aware of. As presented in Chapter 3, most people within the Lean industry translate the Japanese word *kaizen* to "change for the better." Jun Nakamuro, a Lean sensei trained by Taiichi Ohno's protégé, says that "change for the better" is part of kaizen, but not all of it. He suggested that the meaning of kaizen would be better translated as "continuous self-development," something, as demonstrated in the principles, that is fundamental to Marine Corps leadership.

The first principle, "Be technically and tactically proficient," also requires a certain element of self-development. As technologies change and new tactics are learned and developed throughout the military community, it is expected that leaders will seek both of these out and learn and grow themselves. As senior leaders develop their junior leaders, they too will be helping them become more proficient and therefore pushing their troops and junior leaders to learn.

Leadership in the Marines covers more than just learning, but one of the key elements throughout my time in the Marines, and I am certain it continues to this day, is that to be successful, it is not enough to follow rules by rote in all circumstances. People need to be able to think and learn for themselves based on the guiding principles of the organization, whatever they may be. The leaders in the USMC enable this through developing and coaching their Marines.

━━━━━━━━━

PepsiCo

When I joined PepsiCo, they had only just begun thinking about Lean and what it could do for the organization. They, were however, very strong on leadership. Within a few weeks of starting, I was sent to their "Ops Academy," a weeklong program to ensure that new leaders in the organization understood the ethos of how PepsiCo worked. It was very people focused. At PepsiCo, the annual review of each leader was influenced some 40% or 50% by how well the leader "brought others along," which meant developing the people who worked for you to become better, to learn, to develop their skills and abilities.

While they were very focused on results, they were just as focused on how well leaders developed those who worked in their team. PepsiCo had a set of Leadership Imperatives, quite possibly because the principles in PepsiCo were important regardless of your position. The PepsiCo Leadership Imperatives were as follows (Fulmer and Bleak, 2008, p. 42):

- Setting the agenda
- Taking others with you
- Doing it the right way

Taking others with you, as previously mentioned, is about ensuring that you are developing those who work in your team. Accomplishing the objective in PepsiCo is as much about developing your people as it is about the result.

PepsiCo also has six guiding principles. These principles were one of the core themes in this Ops Academy and arguably the main lesson I learned while on the program. Any decision you make while working in PepsiCo should be based on one or more of these principles. As long as you could justify your decision on these principles, your seniors and the organization as a whole would back you up (PepsiCo, 2014).

PepsiCo Guiding Principles

Care for our customers, our consumers, and the world we live in.
Sell only products we can be proud of.
Speak with truth and candor.
Win with diversity and inclusion.
Balance short term and long term.
Respect others and succeed together.

Interestingly, the final two principles can be seen in Toyota's 14 principles; PepsiCo's fifth principle is similar to the first principle at Toyota—"Base your management decisions on a long-term philosophy, even at the expense of short-term financial goals." OK, it's not an exact match, but there is similarity there. But the principle suggests that everyone should consider the long-term impacts of any decision, something that seems to be lacking in so many businesses today.

The first half of the final principle, "Respect others and succeed together," is at the heart of Toyota's Production System. In its simplest form, people can cover the entirety of the Toyota Production System in two phrases, "continuous improvement" and "respect for people."

While the culture at PepsiCo was arguably one of the "softest" I have worked in, it was also very driven. There was a huge expectation that we would not only hit our targets, but that we would take on additional challenges along the way. Regardless of what we had to achieve, though, if we did it at the cost of those who worked in our team, it was as bad as not delivering at all. It simply wasn't a consideration that you wouldn't work with your team and use them and their abilities to deliver the result, and at the same time challenge them and develop their abilities to do more on an ongoing basis.

In the USMC and PepsiCo, as well as Toyota—and I am sure this type of leadership exists elsewhere—the basic premise was that people should follow the rules until they don't make sense, and then challenge the status quo. There are always limits to how far you can go, and more so in some organizations than others; but the general principle is that we should be developing our people to think for themselves. Lean is not the same thing as Taylorism, where we as leaders decide how things should be done. Lean is not about setting standards at the head office and rolling them out to the entire organization. McDonald's, as discussed in Chapter 3, is not Lean. They are efficient, but the engagement from the front line is limited.

Having said that, there is an argument that those who do choose to engage while working at McDonald's, those who decide to stay on and make a career of it, do get a significant amount of development and support. But it will never become an organization with an army of problem solvers. It is unlikely there will ever be a significant amount of autonomy at the front line in McDonald's.

SUMMARY

There is no silver bullet. The best organizations in the world still make mistakes and have problems. Acceptance of this is arguably the first step to true improvement, as well as personal development. Trust is key to enabling people to experiment and make mistakes. Alongside trust is the idea that each experiment is small and will have limited or negligible impact if it goes wrong. But all of this is predicated on the idea that the leadership of an organization is working with their people to coach and to develop them to create better systems, to make problems more obvious, more quickly, and to solve problems at the root cause, not just remove the symptom.

Many organizations say they are good at solving problems, but often, they are not really solving them, just hiding them from either the customer or the senior management. They hide them by creating workarounds, ignoring the rules and standards. They hide them by cooking the books or "creative accounting." Yes, this even happens at the front line: reporting figures that do not reflect the real situation but are more acceptable to a leadership team that is not engaged with the front line but merely wants the numbers to be met day in, day out.

All of this hiding of problems, or solving them merely by removing the symptom, means the organization isn't learning; the individuals aren't learning, or they are learning the wrong things. The problems are growing, slowly at first behind a curtain of opacity. Eventually they will surface, and when they do, the organization won't truly know how to handle them. They haven't built their capability to solve problems when they were small; they didn't create an army of problem solvers who know how to dig deep to truly understand what caused the problem to arise in the first place. There is no willingness for people to admit that someone had mistakenly omitted a step in the process that was mandated from headquarters.

This unwillingness to make mistakes comes from leadership's lack of engagement and working with their team to develop them. The expectation is that you are hired to do a job, not to learn how to do it better. This is a mistaken belief that seems rampant throughout western management thinking. Arguably, it is a result of many of the institutions of capitalism, the idea that individuals are responsible for their own education and development.

This is true to an extent, but the adage of the CFO asking the CEO what happens if we invest in our people and they leave comes to mind—the CEO's response is priceless: "What happens if we don't, and they stay?" This is exactly what is happening in so many businesses today. The organization invests in technology, in consultants, and in new processes, but they seem to avoid or minimize investing in their people.

Maybe this isn't a conscious avoidance, and I'm not suggesting they need to spend huge amounts of money. The best investment in people is time: time spent with leadership coaching and developing the capabilities of people to build systems and processes that make problems obvious; solving problems at the root cause, not just removing the symptom; and sharing knowledge gained along the way. This new knowledge being shared is about the business processes where the problems occurred and about the process of solving the problem. Both can always be improved, and it is through learning and building new knowledge that this happens.

11

What Next?

The HBO series *Westworld* has recently begun airing in the United Kingdom. Having watched the first three episodes, I am certain I heard the same quote in at least two, "Evolution forged the entirety of sentient life on this planet using one tool, the mistake" (HBO, 2016). The problem here is that although nature seems adept at using mistakes to make progress, humankind seems all too happy to ignore the lessons that we should incorporate into our thinking following the mistakes that we make. This applies to individuals as well as society as a whole. We often seem much more concerned about who is to blame than what we should be doing differently as a result of what we learn from the mistakes we make.

Throughout this book, I have attempted to demonstrate that while the tools and techniques within Lean will provide an improved operational capability, it is the capability of the organization to learn that truly sets world-class organizations apart. I have also tried to demonstrate that these same tools, applied with the intention of learning as a higher priority than the improvement of the operation itself, will not only enable this learning within the organization, but it will also provide a consistent approach that can be developed and improved upon. This will further accelerate the organization's ability to grow and move ahead of its competition, setting the pace for their industry.

Many authors have written about the importance of organizational learning. Some organizations are truly exceptional at learning; sadly, they seem too few and far between in my view. Most organizations that begin to use Lean to improve their business focus only on their operation. They ignore the potential for improving every area of their business. Arguably, much of that resistance to doing so comes from the idea that outside of operations is much more knowledge-based work. There are few physical processes, and the tools and techniques people learn when beginning to use Lean are primarily focused on physical processes, like assembly lines.

However, when we move beyond the simplistic view of the Lean tools as mechanisms to remove waste, we begin to understand that they provide much more than that. These tools are ways to make problems obvious; the thinking behind them enables problem solving at the root cause, not just symptom removal. Remember, even waste is a symptom of something else. Waste is not caused by waste; it is caused by poor system design, poor thinking. Yet we must accept that, as Steven Spear (2009) said, "No team can *design* a perfect system in advance, planning for every contingency and nuance. However,...people can *discover* great systems and keep discovering how to make them better" (p. 92).

We must accept that not even the most knowledgeable person in our organization, nor those we bring in to help us, can design perfection; arguably, we cannot achieve perfection. However, we can work toward it; we can work toward greater knowledge of our processes, our systems that underlie them, and the thinking that was used to design them. Throughout this work toward greater knowledge, we will inevitably improve our systems, processes, and thinking as we discover the gaps, limitations, and flaws in our previous thinking.

We must begin to open our eyes to the flaws in the paradigms of old and begin to find new paradigms that enable us to move beyond where we are, and into a new level of performance based on a higher level of understanding and knowledge about what we do and why we do it. Deming (1993), while discussing management of people, said, "We must throw overboard our theories and practices of the present, and build afresh" (p. 121). While there are undoubtedly some things we should hold on to, there are many things we need to let go of. What is most important is the willingness to explore, analyze, and reflect on our own paradigms; are they helping or hurting us, individually and organizationally?

Through active problem solving, where we dig deep to truly understand why these problems arise, we can also learn about ourselves and the fact that we should all be working toward the same objective, achieving greater security for our organizations and hence for ourselves.

The point of all of this: you can continue to use the tools and techniques within Lean to remove waste. You can continue to focus only on bottom line results in the very near future. Or you can begin to create capability for growth, long-term growth.

You create this capability not by copying others or by using what others have used, but by understanding that whatever you buy, beg, borrow, or steal from others is unlikely to be appropriate or sufficient to take you beyond what they have achieved. Deming (1993) wrote, "To copy an example of success, without understanding it with the aid of theory, may lead to disaster." This is because "without theory, there is no learning" (p. 103). Deming was very clear on this: knowledge without theory is merely information. We must have a theory to build knowledge. It is the building of knowledge that will set you apart from others, not the copying of their solutions.

Sure, some may say that even half of what others have achieved is good enough. I can assure you, though, that there are others out there who are not content with that. They are working to be the best, not just as good as others, but the best. This requires moving beyond what others have done and forging the path for yourself.

This path doesn't have to be forged in blindness without a guide, but the guide is not a detailed step-by-step plan to deliver greatness; it is merely a direction to take. Step forward into your future knowing that you will encounter challenges and that you can overcome them.

ON THE BRINK

For those companies that are in dire straits, on the verge of shutting down, or just in a sticky situation that needs to be resolved quickly, then maybe focusing on a few quick wins that will provide breathing room is essential. The learning can come later. However, I would caution against this singular approach even in times of desperation.

For me, this is the burning-platform situation; it is imperative to get off, jump into the unknown, as anything is better than death. That's where the burning-platform analogy came from, a man on a real-life burning platform. However, this limited focus will be hard to switch from once the wider organization begins to understand the intent and purpose behind your Lean initiative, transformation, or whatever you call it. Hopefully, by now, you'll realize the potential damage you can do to the credibility of Lean to the people in your organization.

Once they realize that it is only the latest plan to recover the situation, that your leadership team is not truly engaged with developing your people, they will likely become resistant and reduce the potential improvement. The "What's in it for me?" question is always lingering in the minds of your people. If the answer to that question is "another few months," then the good ones may already be looking elsewhere.

Much better to be clear about the situation, the expectations, and your intent, assuming of course that you understood the message contained within this book. While you may have to take some drastic measures initially, a commitment to immediately shifting focus once that breathing room is obtained will go much further in engaging your workforce to join in your efforts. In my experience, people often don't mind having to pull up the bootstraps and put in a bit of extra effort for a short period if they *know* that it is temporary.

If, however, your intent is to use Lean merely to reduce headcount, to reduce costs, to make the shareholders happy, or worse, to ensure your bonus, then I would ask why you bothered reading this far. Surely nothing written earlier has made any impact on your paradigms for Lean or the flaws of traditional management practices. If this is you, then I would implore you to use a different methodology, or at a minimum, don't call it Lean. We don't need any more examples of companies denigrating Lean by using it to get rid of people!

ALREADY STARTED?

If you have already started and are using a variety of the tools and techniques of Lean, then it is worth taking a pause for thought. Think through what you have done thus far and where it has taken you. How much engagement have you had at each level? Are you focusing on removing waste to create capacity for growth, or are you removing waste to create capacity to enable the reduction of your workforce? Remember, turkeys don't vote for Christmas. You can continue to drive down costs at the expense of your workforce, or you can engage your workforce through a commitment to growth and a commitment to them as individuals.

It is likely that, thus far, your organization has focused predominantly on removing waste. Again, there is nothing wrong with that in and of itself. But it is also insufficient to truly take you beyond the gains that you initially make. True, they may have been large gains, but how much progress have you made since? Is your organization continuing to improve, or have you hit the point of diminishing returns? Are you even sustaining the improvements made to date?

Consider the wasted resource of your front line not engaging, in some cases actually disengaging to the point of subversion. You can have your entire organization pulling together to become a stronger, more flexible, more dynamic organization. Or you can continue to keep the focus on improving operations only, driven predominantly by your management team.

The true value of Lean is not the individual improvements; it is not even the ability to see things differently in your business. The true value of Lean comes from the acceleration of learning through effective problem identification and resolution. The acceleration of the ability to solve problems is essential to deal with the improved flow and reduced waste within your processes.

Many firms have moved to Just in Time (JIT) supply chains or flow lines, or introduced various other Lean concepts, only to find they didn't get the results they expected because they didn't understand how they fit together. They didn't realize that for any of the benefits to be sustained beyond the exit of the consultant requires an organization to be able to effectively solve problems quickly, which in turn requires problems to be highlighted quickly, before they grow too big.

Many try to make the transformation alone; I would advise against this as Deming (1993) did; he wrote that "the transformation requires a view from the outside" (p. 92). This does not mean get a "tool monkey" to help, someone who knows *how* to use the tools but doesn't necessarily understand how they all fit together. Worse still, they know how it all fits together but do not have the ability to truly challenge you and your paradigms. They merely focus on the processes and getting your operation streamlined. These are the folks who "Lean out an area," Often without any real knowledge gained by your people, who are then expected to sustain the improved performance afterward.

What is needed is a coach, a proper coach who understands not just the tools, the techniques, and how they all fit together, but also understands the requirement for learning. The requirement to develop people to think for themselves and build new knowledge within the organization is unquestionable. Depending on the size of your organization and the pace of change you wish to achieve, you may need several coaches at various levels and/or areas of your organization. Yes, it may cost more initially, but this is investment in the long-term growth of your organization, not just a few months' or maybe a year's worth of improvements but a new system based on a new culture.

Almost all professional athletes have coaches. Many amateur athletes have coaches. While it may be obvious why amateurs have coaches, ask yourself why it is that these professionals need a coach. Why do so many sports teams have multiple coaches?

They provide that view from the outside. They provide the challenge to you, your paradigms, and your processes that is unlikely to be found within. They have the time to deeply study your processes and your organizational culture. They can identify the early adapters to help build the coalition of leadership required to make your transformation last. They truly understand the benefits of a learning organization over one that just has good (or even great) processes.

HAVEN'T STARTED YET?

If you haven't begun on your Lean journey, obviously I'm going to suggest a coach again. Yes, most of you are seeing right through my thinly veiled punt at salesmanship. Honestly, though, there are plenty of very good coaches out there providing sound advice and instruction to help organizations move beyond traditional Lean into learning organizations. If your organization is not one that produces assembled products on an assembly line, the preference of a coach over a tool monkey should be obvious. Coaches will help you think differently instead of just do things differently. They understand the thinking behind the tools and how they can benefit your organization with appropriate modification to suit what it is you do.

Besides a coach, I believe it is imperative that leaders in organizations do sufficient research to truly understand what they are embarking on. My colleagues, through anecdotal evidence, and I have seen far too many leaders of organizations begin their journey without fully understanding the implications for themselves. One of the biggest misconceptions I have seen is that because we are reducing waste, therefore making the work easier, better, faster, and cheaper, things will also be easier for the leadership. Actually, this is often the opposite of what you should expect. Managing the systems through the development of your people takes a significant amount of effort and learning on your part.

This is not just about the mechanics of running a Lean business model but also about the necessary cultural norms, interpersonal relationship norms, and the required level of commitment to the development of your people that often create more work for the senior people, initially at least. This is because very few, if any, organizations are prepared to let go of old practices as soon as they start. They often hold on to old reporting processes, authorization processes, and all manner of unnecessary bureaucracy because they are unsure of what will replace it, if anything.

In addition to the new work seemingly on top of the old, there is a significant amount of learning to be done. I've already mentioned Ohno's belief that the teacher must be learning in advance of the student. As a leader in your organization, you must be learning and building your knowledge as fast or faster than your people, because it is you who will be teaching them. You will not be teaching them what you learned in business school but what you are learning in the process of coaching them and creating systems and processes that make problems obvious. You will be learning and then teaching about solving problems and the methods to do so. You will be guiding them to share the knowledge they gain with their peers and subordinates.

All the while, this learning and teaching will pick up pace, gain breadth across your organization until you create a snowball of learning that carries on under its own weight. If you do this right, you will have created a culture where people are focused on making things better, for themselves and the organization. They will do this improvement in a focused and structured manner with the clear expectation of learning at each step.

Finally, be clear on what you want to achieve. This should not be about greater profits; they will come, but they are not the focus. This should not be about beating the competition; that too will come. Where do you see your organization 5 or 10 years from now? What about 50 years? This is about what Deming called "constancy of purpose," about ensuring the future of your organization by preparing it to deal with the future, whatever that may be.

You can prepare yourself and your organization for whatever may come, or you can continue to think that where you are now is sufficient. The annals of history are filled with the failures of arrogance, where people thought they were good enough. They may have been for that time, but as time moves on, they followed in the footsteps of all the others who refused to learn.

TRAINING PROGRAMS

There is nothing wrong with the principle of going down the training route. There are many good programs and courses available. However, sending a handful of people to a weeklong course that teaches the tools will have little if any effect in your organization. Sending a bunch of front-line folks on a course only to find they have limited if any support afterward is a waste of money. However, if you send a large enough number of your leaders on appropriate courses with the intention of building a leading coalition of advocates, then you're getting closer to the mark.

Ideally, any course needs to be an immersive experience, not an academic classroom-based program but one where there are opportunities to apply the knowledge during the course. There should be opportunities to challenge and build on what is being taught. These should be real-life activities coupled with simulations, some as separate activities and some integral to the program.

Any course needs to have sufficient length to provide enough absorption for your people to feel the difference in leadership behaviors required to begin coaching their people. They don't need to become experts in the tools; they need to learn how to think for themselves and use the principles behind the tools to start affecting change.

Realistically, you will need several courses to get through sufficient numbers to build that coalition. After each course, the attendees should immediately put what they learned into practice; many organizations require a short project or experiment. While the focus on these projects or experiments should be about bedding in the learning, in most cases, they also deliver a return to the business. Ideally, these folks will continue to receive some coaching, guidance, and support as they begin to apply their learning. Initially, this is likely to come from an external coach. Wherever possible, these immediate experiments should include members of their team to begin practicing the coaching as well as the application of what was learned. The opportunity to set the wheels in motion will never be as good as immediately after the first knowledge transfer.

Through periodic reviews with them and their coach, covering progress, learning, and development, you will be able to see how they have been able to incorporate the principles into new routines, new thinking about how they contribute to the organization, new behaviors in their interactions with others, and how they have begun developing their people through coaching.

In time, with sufficient momentum and enough advocates to sustain the right behaviors, the organization will begin to see improvements hitting the bottom line as people begin using their knowledge, skills, and talent to improve their knowledge, skills, and talent while improving your organization. This sharpening of the saw, the self-improvement that comes from greater knowledge, will eventually become a sustainable platform on which you will continue to build new knowledge.

FINAL THOUGHTS

Our application of Lean over the years has been incorrectly focused on tools, techniques, and quick returns on investment. If we move beyond the tools and techniques and begin using our brains for thinking and learning, not just doing, we will gain much more than we have thus far. The business world is crying out for productivity gains; sadly, the focus is too much on headcounts and technology.

When I began toying with the idea of writing this book some years ago, I had a very different thought process for what it would include and why I would write it. I began putting things down on paper, and as I did, I realized that I still had so much to learn. The ideas continued, and occasionally, I would open up the file; add a few more lines, a new chapter; and occasionally start over, completely.

As I come to the end of writing this, I now realize that what I thought I needed to learn was a drop in the ocean compared to what I now want to learn. I have gained so much new knowledge in this process, yet part of that is the amount of learning still to do. I have become the consciously incompetent—because if I claimed to be competent, then I may slip into the belief that I don't need to keep learning!

Nokia virtually replaced Motorola in the late 1990s. They went quickly to the top because they were ready to go digital when Motorola was still working on achieving Six Sigma-level quality. The market just wanted digital, even with the bugs.

However, what Nokia weren't able to do was keep up with the changes. After the press release announcing the purchase of Nokia by Microsoft, Rahul Gupta (2016) wrote, "Nokia has been a respectable company. They didn't do anything wrong in their business, however, the world changed too fast. Their opponents were too powerful. *They missed out on learning,* they missed out on changing, and thus they lost the opportunity at hand to make it big" (emphasis added).

You too can make it big in a short time; you can have great quarters and even great years. If you want to have a great career and leave a legacy, you'll have to put sufficient focus into doing what Nokia was accused of not doing—thinking and learning!

Appendix: A Selection of Tools and Techniques and How They Support *See, Solve, Share,* and *Show*

Tool/Technique	See	Solve	Share	Show
5S	X	X	X	X
Andon		X		X
Bottleneck analysis		X		X
Continuous flow	X			X
Gemba (the real place)	X			X
Heijunka (level scheduling)	X			X
Hoshin Kanri (policy deployment)	X			X
Jidoka (autonomation)	X	X		X
Jishuken		X		X
Just in Time (JIT)	X			X
Kaizen (continuous improvement)		X		X
Kamishibai	X		X	X
Kanban (pull system)	X	X	X	X
Key performance indicators (KPIs)	X	X		X
Muda (waste)	X		X	X
Overall equipment effectiveness (OEE)	X	X	X	X
Plan–do–check–act (PDCA)		X	X	X
Poka yoke (error proofing)	X	X		X
Process confirmation	X		X	X
Root cause analysis		X		X
Single-Minute Exchange of Die (SMED)	X			X
Six big losses	X	X		X
SMART goals	X	X		X
Standardized work	X	X	X	X
Takt time	X			X
Total Productive Maintenance (TPM)	X	X		X
Value Stream Mapping	X	X	X	X
Visual factory	X		X	X
Yokoten	X		X	X

Bibliography

Armstrong, P. 2016. Bloom's taxonomy. Center for Teaching. https://cft.vanderbilt.edu /guides-sub-pages/blooms-taxonomy/

Balle, M., Godefroy, B., Smalley, A. & Sobek, D. K. 2006. The thinking production system. *Reflections*. Vol. 7, No. 2, pp. 1–12, http://artoflean.com/files/ThinkingProduction System.pdf

Barker, J. A. 2001. The new business of paradigms. http://ocw.metu.edu.tr/pluginfile .php/3298/course/section/1177/TranscriptClassicPreview_NBOP.pdf

Bashō, M. (n.d.). Do Not Follow in the Footsteps of the Wise. http://english.stackexchange .com/questions/280014/do-not-seek-to-follow-in-the-footsteps-of-the-wise

BD. 2016. Standards. http://www.businessdictionary.com/definition/standards.html

Berfield, S. 2015. Why It's So Hard for McDonald's to Change. *Bloomberg*. http://www.bloom berg.com/news/articles/2015-01-29/why-it-s-so-hard-for-mcdonald-s-to-change

Branson, R. C. N. 2014. Staff come first. *Virgin Website*. https://www.virgin.com /richard-branson/staff-come-first

Buchanan, R. T. 2015. McDonalds to close more stores than it opens in US for first time in 40 years. *The Independent Online*. http://www.independent.co.uk/news/world /mcdonalds-to-close-more-stores-than-it-opens-in-us-for-first-time-in-40-years -10333642.html

Deming, W. E. 1982. *Out of the Crisis*. Cambridge, MA: MIT Press.

Deming, W. E. 1993. *The New Economics*. Cambridge, MA: MIT Press.

Dixon. J. (n.d.). Quotery. http://www.quotery.com/quotes/if-you-focus-on-results-you -will-never-change-if/

Dunn, K. 2008. Can This Turnover Number from McDonalds (44%) Be Right? *Fistful of Talent*. http://fistfuloftalent.com/2008/05/can-this-turnov.html

Emiliani, M. L. & Seymour, P. J. 2011. Frank George Woollard: Forgotten pioneer of flow production. *Journal of Management History*. Vol. 17, No. 1, pp. 66–87.

Flinchbaugh, J. & Carlino, A. 2006. *The Hitchhiker's Guide to Lean; Lessons from the Road*. Dearborn, MI: Society of Manufacturing Engineers.

Fuda, P. 2012. *Fire Metaphor: From 'Burning Platform' to 'Burning Ambition' (Leadership Transformation)*. Retrieved October 20, 2016 from https://www.youtube.com /watch?v=Tfn6vD4yyC4

Fulmer, R. M. & Bleak, J. L. 2008. *The Leadership Advantage: How the Best Companies Are Developing Their Talent to Pave the Way for Future Success*. New York: American Management Association.

Godin, S. 2008. *Tribes*. London: Hachette.

Goldratt, E. J. & Cox, J. 1984. *The Goal*. New York: Routledge.

Gorman, B. A. 1979. Discover Eli Whitney. Remarkable City: Industrial New Haven and the Nation, 1800–1900. http://teachersinstitute.yale.edu/curriculum/units/1979/3/79.03 .03.x.html

Gupta, R. 2016. Nokia CEO ended his speech saying this "we didn't do anything wrong, but somehow, we lost." https://www.linkedin.com/pulse/nokia-ceo-ended-his -speech-saying-we-didnt-do-anything-rahul-gupta?trk=hp-feed-article-title-like

Hammer, M. 1990. Reengineering work: Don't automate, obliterate. *Harvard Business Review*, Vol. 68, No. 4, pp. 104–112. https://hbr.org/1990/07/reengineering-work -dont-automate-obliterate

Hayes, R. H., Wheelwright, S. C. & Clark, K. B. 1988. *Dynamic Manufacturing: Creating the Learning Organization*. New York: Free Press.

HBO. 2016. *Westworld*. http://www.magicalquote.com/series/westworld/page/4/

Hoffer, E. 1973. Eric Hoffer quotes. http://erichoffer.blogspot.co.uk/

Johnston, C. (n.d.). The Hierarchy of Tools. Kaizen Consulting and Training Services (KCTS) Ltd. Training Material.

Juran, J. 1964. *Managerial Breakthrough*. New York: McGraw-Hill.

Kiechel, W. 2012. The management century. *Harvard Business Review*, Vol. 90, No. 11, pp. 62–75, 148. https://hbr.org/2012/11/the-management-century

Kjærulff, H. 2016. The 5i Approach to Daily Problem Solving. https://www.linkedin.com /pulse/5i-approach-daily-problem-solving-henrik-kj%C3%A6rulff?trk=mp-reader -card

Lareau, W. 2000. *Lean Leadership*. Carmel, IN: Kaufman Consulting Group.

Li, J. X., Bevan, A., Martinon-Torres, M., Rehren, T., Cao, W., Xia, Y. & Zhao, K. 2014. Crossbows and imperial craft organisation: The bronze triggers of China's Terracotta Army. https://www.academia.edu/6231568/Crossbows_and_imperial _craft_organisation_the_bronze_triggers_of_China_s_Terracotta_Army_Li_et _al_2014_Antiquity_?auto=download

Lienhard, J. H. 1997. No. 1252: Interchangeable Parts. Engines of Our Ingenuity. http:// www.uh.edu/engines/epi1252.htm

Maxwell, J. C. 1999. *The 21 Indispensable Qualities of a Leader*. Nashville, TN: Nelson.

McManis, L. 2016. *The Iceberg of Ignorance Debunked*. http://www.thinkwaystrategies .com/iceberg-ignorance-debunked

Miller, R. 2013. A continuing lean journey: The Shingo Prize at 25—Discovering the power of principles in culture change. http://www.lean.org/common/display/?o=2257

Moen, R. D. & Norman, C. L. 2010. Circling back: Clearing up myths about the Deming cycle and seeing how it keeps evolving. *Quality Progress*. http://apiweb.org/circling-back.pdf

Mooers, C. N. 1996. Mooers' law or why some retrieval systems are used and others are not. *Bulletin of the American Society for Information Science and Technology*, Vol. 23, pp. 22–23.

Morgan, J. M. & Liker, J. K. 2006. *The Toyota Product Development System*. New York: Productivity Press.

Nakamura, J. 2016. Kaizen: Lost in Translation. https://www.linkedin.com/pulse /kaizen-lost-translation-jun-nakamuro-1?trk=hp-feed-article-title-comment

Nakane, J. & Hall, R. A. 2002. Ohno's Method, Creating a Survival Work Culture. *Target*, Vol. 18, No. 1, pp. 6–15. http://www.ame.org/sites/default/files/target_articles/02-18 -1-Ohnos_Method.pdf

Nietzsche, F. W., 1844–1900. 1998. *Twilight of the Idols or How to Philosophize with a Hammer*. New York: Oxford University Press.

Ohno, T. 2006. Ask 'why' five times about every matter. http://www.toyota-global.com /company/toyota_traditions/quality/mar_apr_2006.html

Ohno, T. 2013. *Workplace Management*. New York: McGraw-Hill.

Oxford. 2016. Standards. http://www.oxforddictionaries.com/definition/english/standard

PepsiCo. 2014. PepsiCo Global Code of Conduct. https://www.pepsico.com/Assets /Download/CodeOfConduct/English_GCOC_2014.pdf

Pink, D. 2009a. The Surprising Science of Motivation. https://www.ted.com/talks/dan_pink_on_motivation?language=en

Pink, D. 2009b. *Drive: The Surprising Truth about What Motivates Us.* New York: Riverhead Books.

Pinsen, D. 2016. Danaher: Better Than Berkshire Hathaway? http://seekingalpha.com/article/3994096-danaher-better-berkshire-hathaway

Quote Investigator. 2014. It Is Not the Strongest of the Species that Survives But the Most Adaptable. http://quoteinvestigator.com/2014/05/04/adapt/

Roser, J. 2015. 230 Years of Interchangeable Parts—A Brief History. http://www.allaboutlean.com/230-years-interchangeability/

Senge, P. M. 1990. *The Fifth Discipline: The Art and Practice of the Learning Organization.* London: Century Business.

Shewhart, W. A. 1939. *Statistical Method from the Viewpoint of Quality Control.* Washington, DC: U.S. Department of Agriculture.

Sinek, S. 2009. How great leaders inspire action. https://www.ted.com/talks/simon_sinek_how_great_leaders_inspire_action?language=en

Snapp, S. 2012. Who was the first to engage in mass production? Ford or the Venetians? http://www.scmfocus.com/productionplanningandscheduling/2012/07/04/who-was-the-first-to-engage-in-mass-production-ford-or-the-venetians/

Spear, S. 2004. Learning to lead at Toyota. *Harvard Business Review.* Vol. 82, No. 5, pp. 78–86, https://hbr.org/2004/05/learning-to-lead-at-toyota

Spear, S. J. 2009. *The High-Velocity.* New York: McGraw-Hill.

Spear, S. J. & Bowen, H. K. 1999. Decoding the DNA of Toyota. *Harvard Business Review,* Vol. 77, No. 5, pp. 96–106, https://hbr.org/1999/09/decoding-the-dna-of-the-toyota-production-system

Strategos Inc. (n.d.). Pioneers of lean manufacturing: Taiichi Ohno and Shigeo Shingo. http://www.strategosinc.com/downloads/lean_pioneers-dl1.pdf

Taleb, N. N. 2012. *AntiFragile—Things that Gain from Disorder.* New York: Random House.

Taylor, F. W. 1911. *The Principles of Scientific Management.* New York: Harper & Brothers Publishers.

Toyota Website. 2012. 75 Years of Toyota. http://www.toyota-global.com/company/history_of_toyota/75years/text/index.html

von Moltke, H. 2009. *Moltke on the Art of War.* Edited by Hughes, D. J. New York: Presidio Press.

Vlaskovits, P. 2011. Henry Ford, innovation, and that "faster horse" quote. *Harvard Business Review.* https://hbr.org/2011/08/henry-ford-never-said-the-fast

Waring, N. 2005. What is the difference between Toyota and the rest of the automotive world? MBA Thesis, University of Cardiff.

Womack, J. P., Jones, D. T. & Roos D. 2007. *The Machine that Changed the World.* London: Simon & Schuster.

Wikipedia. 2016. United States Marine Corps. https://en.wikipedia.org/wiki/United_States_Marine_Corps#Budget

Ziglar, Z. 2015. People builders. https://www.ziglar.com/quotes/business-people/

Index

Page numbers followed by f indicate figures.